GROUNDSWELL
STORIES OF SAVING PLACES, FINDING COMMUNITY

GROUNDSWELL

STORIES OF SAVING PLACES, FINDING COMMUNITY

ALIX W. HOPKINS

THE TRUST *for* PUBLIC LAND

CONSERVING LAND FOR PEOPLE

ISBN: 978-1-932807-04-2

Book and cover design: Tom Morgan and Laura McBride,
Blue Design, Portland, Maine

Printed in Hong Kong

10 9 8 7 6 5 4 3 2 1

The Trust for Public Land
116 New Montgomery, 4th Floor
San Francisco, CA 94105

(415) 495-4014
(415) 495-0540 (fax)

The author wishes to acknowledge, with gratitude, the
co-sponsorship of:
The Conservation Fund
The National Park Service Rivers & Trails Program
The Nature Conservancy

For C. A. Porter Hopkins—my earliest inspiration

"Not only is another world possible, she is on her way. On a quiet day, I can hear her breathing." —Arundhati Roy

CONTENTS

FOREWORD

Senator George J. Mitchell

Groundswell: Saving Places, Finding Community offers six stories of how people build a greater sense of community in the process of saving the land on which their lives, livelihoods, and legacies are grounded. In my own experience, the passion for "place" that defines a community is often the key element for achieving surprising agreement and positive results. From my earliest days growing up in a multiethnic mill town in Maine to becoming majority leader of the United States Senate, I learned that I could get much more done by working with others than I could accomplish alone. This ability helped me to facilitate the historic agreement between the two hostile communities in Northern Ireland. The conflicts there, in the Middle East, and in the Balkans all involve competing territorial claims: ownership and use of land. But love of land can generate cooperation as well as conflict.

When Alix Hopkins asked me to write the foreword for this book, I remembered her collegial leadership style at Portland Trails in Maine during the 1990s. The organization grew and prospered for several reasons. The idea was compelling—connecting people to trails and parks in Portland, along its extensive waterfront and undiscovered natural areas. The synergy was strong—among citizens, elected officials, civic

LEFT: Along Montana's Rocky Mountain Front.

and social groups, schools and corporate interests. And, as founding executive director, Alix possessed the ability to organize and guide an abundance of talented local people to do what they did best. Here was grassroots participation in its most effective form. The stories in this book, including Portland Trails, explore the relationships between people and the land for which they care so deeply. When people work collectively on projects to benefit their communities and the environment, they come away with much more than they originally expected. They create lasting connections and develop greater respect for differing opinions. Often they enjoy the process so much that they take on bigger challenges. Learning about their skills and strengths, they join local committees, perhaps even run for office. In short, they contribute to democracy in America in the truest sense.

You can undertake this work where you live. Whether you are interested in learning more about park, trail, river, forest, ranch, or farm projects—large or small—you will find pertinent and inspiring stories in this book. Read them and re-make them for the benefit of yourself and your own community. The results may not be exactly as you initially envisioned, but they will likely extend beyond your wildest imagining. In a world where so much is uncertain, we must find ways to engage in positive undertakings that make a difference where we live—and in the places we love.

—*George J. Mitchell served for fourteen years in the U.S. Senate, including six as majority leader. He then chaired the Northern Ireland peace negotiation and, subsequently, the International Committee on Violence in the Middle East.*

INTRODUCTION

In today's increasingly fast-paced, high-tech world, people long for a sense of community, for connections to one another and to natural places of peace and beauty. Quietly, and for more than twenty years, a growing network of community trails, riverfront parks, forests, farms, and gardens have satisfied this hunger, offering welcome refuges in neighborhoods, rural towns, and cities across the country. Along the way, the people responsible for these endeavors have benefited far more than merely by accomplishing their original goals. In a very tangible way, the process of collaborative, community-based conservation builds better democracy and creates more compassionate citizens to practice it. It opens up the possibility of a shared future for those of us who live in this ever more isolating society.

The inspiration for *Groundswell* springs from my transforming experience at the helm of Portland Trails, a nonprofit organization in Portland, Maine, that began as an urban trails-oriented land trust in the early 1990s. In just a few years, we became an integral part of community life for people of all ages, sizes, and ethnic and economic backgrounds. Who could have known that Portland Trails would grow to encompass so much? Yet, while working together to accomplish our vision for a citywide, thirty-mile trail network, we made lasting friendships and discovered our collective

LEFT: A rendering by C. Michael Lewis helps to spark interest in the possibilities for a harborfront trail along the Eastern Promenade in Portland, Maine.

strengths and individual skills. Then, having found both our voices and ourselves, a good many of us rose to higher levels of activism and responsibility—in work, in civic service, and in political venues.

Certain places in my life have always inspired my passion, and therefore I feel blessed to have found my calling in the land conservation world. Yet some intangible, more meaningful ingredient was missing from my work until I became executive director of Portland Trails. There I learned *firsthand* the power of building a stronger community by directly engaging people to help in a variety of ways. The process changed my life and helped me realize my potential to accomplish things I'd never imagined possible. This revelation came not from others praising me but from my own experience in an expanding leadership role. At Portland Trails we built lasting connections with citizens, political officials, corporations, and civic groups; schools, artists, and professionals; local, state, regional, and federal agencies; and the media—just about anyone interested in or helpful to achieving our mission. You can read more about our story in this book.

Upon leaving Portland Trails after almost eight years, I felt it important to share my insights and to try to empower others wanting to save the special places in their own communities. For four years I've sought out inspirational role models in community-based conservation initiatives and the people who made them happen. The result is a book that covers six projects in locations across the country, chosen intuitively rather than intellectually. The people involved in these projects share the qualities of curiosity, courage, creativity, humor, and perseverance; key to each story are elements of synchronicity, timing, collaboration, and strong leadership. It is my hope that the examples chosen will both inspire and provide practical information for those who want to lead the charge in their own communities. To me, the "how" and the "why" of project genesis are inextricably interwoven, enabling most any vision to succeed.

Following the stories, the section entitled Stepping Stones will help answer many commonly asked questions. The Resources section offers links, contacts, and project information for featured organizations and initiatives.

Faced with the difficulty of finding an appropriate "second act" to my affirming experience at Portland Trails, I soon realized that the journey I embarked upon while writing this book would offer a follow-up gift. My travels took me from Portland, Maine, to the Bronx River in New York City; from Washington State to coastal North Carolina; from a Wisconsin farm to the Rocky Mountains of Montana. The opportunity to meet with so many people from such diverse geographic, cultural, and class backgrounds has opened my eyes to new ways of creating relevant and resonant land conservation, while confirming my convictions about the transcendent power of community-based work.

The Bronx River in New York City is a place where people—often with modest beginnings—realized their potential as community activists through participating in a river restoration effort. Many involved have gone on to become outspoken advocates for environmental, economic, and social equality in their long-neglected Bronx neighborhoods. In Bellingham, Washington, a small land trust partnered with two timber companies, the county parks and recreation department, the local university, and a national land conservation organization to accomplish a remarkable feat. Raising more than $4 million to preserve a threatened stand of ancient, thousand-year-old trees, they created a new community forest and built a beautiful trail winding through it to a ridgetop with spectacular views. As a result of their efforts, the Canyon Lake Creek Community Forest will be enjoyed by county residents for recreational and education purposes for generations to come. In Columbia, North Carolina, a visionary economic development plan focused on using a rural county's natural and cultural resources to attract, for the first time, tourists passing on their way to the famed Outer Banks beach resorts. As part of this project, whites and African-Americans collaborated in unprecedented fashion to create greater economic opportunities and social value for all residents. Families in Minneapolis and St. Paul, Minnesota, bought annual shares of produce from a farm located an hour and a state away, in Osceola, Wisconsin. As members of a community-supported agriculture project, they connected themselves firmly to the land as the source of their food while preserving a farming family's livelihood. Lastly, I visited Montana, along the Rocky Mountain Front, where the Great Plains collide with the eastern slope of the Rockies. Here I learned anew about the depth of people's love for their land and way of life from ranchers fighting to stay close to the roots laid down by earlier generations. They accomplished this by using collective action and practical solutions, and by developing genuine respect and affection for one another, regardless of whether or not they were former adversaries.

I have always suspected that the passion of individuals for the places they live is the fundamental catalyst behind community-based land conservation; this feeling was profoundly confirmed when I met Majora Carter. Despite my inclinations as a people person, I remember feeling anxious before visiting this

Such kindred spirits are legion across the country—wherever there are people who care about their community, there are people who will embrace the notion of collaboration.

Bronx native who became an accomplished leader largely through participating in the Bronx River Restoration Project—learning in the process about her strengths, and encouraging others to accompany her. Whatever might Majora and I share? She had grown up in the ghetto, transcending humble origins to obtain graduate degrees and direct the nonprofit Sustainable South Bronx. I had grown up relatively privileged on a farm in Maryland. But after I recounted my pivotal tenure at the helm of Portland Trails to her, she replied, "When you described your own experience, I got goose bumps. The very same thing happened to me!" Our common understanding and love of place gave us the realization that we shared a new language of empowerment.

Such kindred spirits are legion across the country—wherever there are people who care about their community, there are people who will embrace the notion of collaboration. We need to find each other and help each other to succeed. That is why I've written this book.

Whether you are considering creating a riverfront trail or protecting a beloved parcel of open space, such as an historic farm or forest in your town, it is my hope that you will find a story here to inspire you to move forward with your own good ideas. Do not be deterred by the complexities involved or the frustration of inevitable delays. If you are reading this, you are already on your way. As I heard over and over again from those I met, showing up is half the battle. And if not us, who will do this work?

So get going!

Alix W. Hopkins

LEFT: Black bear tracks on the beach at the Palmetto-Peartree Preserve, Tyrrell County, North Carolina.

"We didn't really start Portland Trails. It lay dormant in the weeds, bushes, old towpaths,

and abandoned rail lines. As soon as someone had the idea, Portland Trails sprang to life."

—Dick Spencer, attorney, conservationist and co-founder

1

PORTLAND TRAILS

Portland, Maine—*Committed citizens give life and form to a century-old vision of linked parks, shorelines, and natural land by creating a system of trails across a small city in the Northeast.*

This is a story about vision, timing, and leadership. In the early 1990s this urban trails-oriented organization struck a chord with people in Portland, Maine, becoming the catalyst for achieving a century-old vision to link city parks and shorelines with a network of trails. Working with the remarkable collection of talented and committed individuals to help give Portland Trails life and form was a rare privilege and a transforming experience for me. It helped me find my calling, and, quite simply, it changed my life.

If you were a bird, you would have a great view of the trail system in Portland, Maine, linking the City's extensive shorelines, parks, and natural areas. If you started at the Stroudwater River Trail, along the western edge, you'd pass a number of historic sites where several centuries ago, giant pines were turned into masts for wooden sailing ships. Moving next to the Fore River Trail, for a time you'd be alongside a now-defunct canal system built by men and mules in the 1800s, stretching from Sebago Lake to the Atlantic Ocean. The trail parallels the marshland along the riverbank and rounds the peninsula toward Portland Harbor, where huge tankers and lobster boats

LEFT: A bird's-eye view of the Portland Peninsula.

alike unload their cargoes in the heart of Portland's downtown commercial district. Next, you'd meet the scenic, two-mile harborfront Eastern Prom Trail, a former rail yard almost developed into condos and a marina in the 1980s. Continuing along the waterfront and under Interstate 295 at Tukey's Bridge, you'd hit the circular, four-mile Back Cove Trail, the hub of the trail system. If it were winter you'd need to stay vigilant—Arctic owls are known to congregate at that time to feast on the plentiful supply of sea ducks. In summer, you'd have to contend with board sailors and lobstermen using the tidal pond for their own purposes. From Back Cove you could branch out in several directions toward any number of other trails.

Most of this work has been accomplished during the past decade.

Founded in the 1600s, Portland is Maine's largest city, with a regional metropolitan population of 300,000. This significant seaport peninsula is bounded by historic waterways, making it a transportation hub for shipping and railroads.

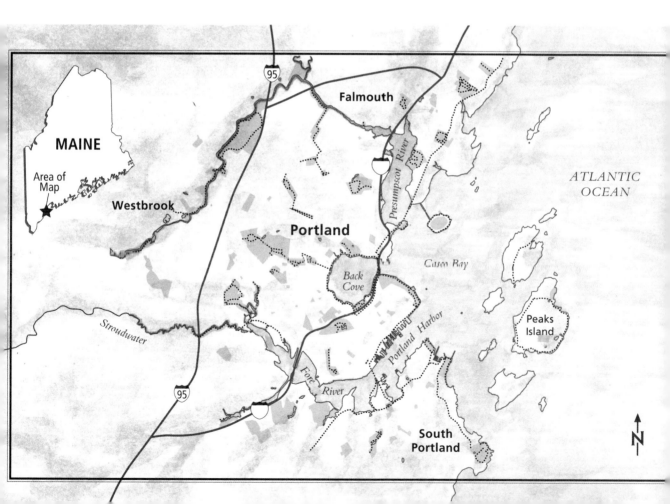

BELOW: A historic photo of a Portland park showing turn-of-the-century craftsmanship and attention to detail.

Portland, Me., Shelter House, Deering Oaks.

P-66361

From Back Cove—the scenic tidal pond—a panoramic vista showcases the surrounding city. From there the navigable Fore River and its commercial waterfront stretch inland to connect with several millstream tributaries, including the Stroudwater River.

After suffering a series of economic downturns and the demolition of several landmark railroad buildings in the latter half of the twentieth century, Portland's fortunes realigned in the early 1990s. Progressive government policies, strong municipal support, new federal trail funding, and solid community leadership coalesced. In this atmosphere Portland Trails (PT) emerged. Only, it grew to encompass more than anyone could have imagined.

A hundred years ago the firm of renowned landscape architect Frederick Law Olmsted designed many of Portland's parks—Deering Oaks, the Eastern and Western Promenades, and Baxter Boulevard, which the planners envisioned linking with trails. But not until the late 1980s, when the city council passed the Shoreway Access Plan, did Olmsted's idea to promote greater citizen access to the city's extensive river and harborfront shorelines, open spaces, and parks get revived. It was put into place by way of a committee of people representing public and private interests, facilitated by Terrence J. DeWan & Associates, a local landscape architectural firm.

Immediately following the council vote to approve the plan, a group of people gathered in the hallway outside the council chamber to talk about how to keep things moving. These citizen activists knew they needed to take action if the plan's goals were ever to become reality. Without a clear purpose and a community effort to drive it, the plan would likely have gathered dust on a shelf, like many other laudable efforts.

Fortunately the group began to get organized right away, meeting at first in various people's living rooms to discuss their goals and the strategies for reaching them. To best carry out the Shoreway Access Plan, the group envisioned creating a trails-oriented urban land trust. Incorporated several years later in 1991, this community-based nonprofit would become the chief vehicle for implementing the collective vision for a thirty-mile trail network linking parks, shorelines, and social centers across the city. "The Shoreway Access Plan turned a light on to illuminate the vision" for Portland Trails, claims co-founder Nathan Smith. "Once we visualized how the city would look with a system of trails, everybody got it," adds co-founder Dick Spencer. "It had the feeling of inevitability. It fed into so many things that existed in people's consciousness but lacked a vehicle through which to act."

The early Portland Trails board included Spencer, Smith, and co-founder Tom Jewell, three highly capable volunteers, lawyers all. Spencer was Portland Trails' first president and resident visionary. He brought a wealth of knowledge about land conservation, politics, and municipal law. Smith, a housing advocate who became PT's second president, has negotiated for some of Portland Trails' most significant projects. Jewell grew up in Portland. His vast local knowledge, coming from a lifetime of exploring the city's wild places, combined with his

vision for trail building, was a treasure without compare. The three set about finding other volunteers eager to help with the mounting workload.

Curiously, finding an appropriate name for the new organization proved challenging for the founding board members. The first two attempts—the Shoreway Access Coalition and the Forest City Land Trust—lacked a certain distinctive ring. The third—Portland Trails—said it all, providing the clear advantage of having the name and the mission all at once.

By late 1991 the group had hired part-time coordinator Donna Larson to work with a small, committed band of supporters to create PT's first membership brochure, among other organizational tasks. The theme, "Take a Hike in the Forest City," was taken from the name given to Portland in honor of the majestic elms and other trees lining the streets during the previous century. Coupled with the catchy name and compelling vision map, the brochure got PT off to a rousing start. Board members mailed it to their friends, immediately gathering fifty members. Although Donna Larson left soon after to follow her career path as a planner, she made a worthy start-up contribution and remained a consistent supporter.

Full-Time Staff

By early 1992 the board realized that fulfilling its mission would require full-time staff. That was where I came in. I vividly recall my first day as executive director in the summer of 1992. Sitting on the floor of our new but empty office, surrounded by all the file boxes left me by relieved volunteers, I thought, "Well, honey, you've talked your way into this job. What in the world do you do now?" I wondered, too, whether the job might ever entail much more than spreading gravel on the ground and whether I had made a huge mistake by limiting myself to a job focusing on trail building. I, of course, had no idea that Portland Trails would transform my life.

PT's third president, after two of the "founding fathers" took their turn, was Peter Monro, a landscape designer, author, editor, and unique creative spirit. He and I muddled through those early days, finding that we worked well together. We called to introduce ourselves to everyone suggested to us—a time-consuming practice that reaped long-term benefits as we slowly began to build relationships with people, businesses, agencies, and other nonprofit organizations in the Portland area. Working with the board, we also created a mission statement: to create a thirty-mile network of multiuse trails within Greater Portland; to serve as a public advocate for the protection of and access to natural places within the region; and to encourage the participation of neighborhoods, schools, and the business community in trail use and stewardship.

Early on, we concentrated on finding diverse, creative, energetic, up-and-coming people to help as board members, rather than tapping individuals who sat on numerous or established organization boards.

At times during those early days, the board and I joked about our heavy slant toward the legal profession, but over the ensuing years, people with complementary skills and interests joined as well. The truth is, more than a dozen attorneys have made invaluable contributions to Portland Trails over the past ten years. Their understanding of legal requirements and real estate, combined with their practical knowledge of how to get things done in Portland—and their associations with people of influence—were pivotal to the organization's success.

Early on, we concentrated on finding diverse, creative, energetic, up-and-coming people to help as board members, rather than tapping individuals who sat on numerous or established organization boards. Because Portland Trails was young, the board clearly needed to reflect our lean, hungry, and maverick vision. To help us we chose to bring on "doers"—people possessing time, enthusiasm, and energy—and not so much the "deep-pockets" crowd. We also made board members feel comfortable about moving on to another cause or focus when the time was right. This ebb and flow made for an especially dynamic, effective board. We tried to recruit people as soon as we recognized their potential. My record was inviting one person to join about fifteen minutes after meeting him; my intuition told me he'd make a great addition—and I was right.

To complement the earlier-mentioned attorneys, PT engaged writers, scientists, engineers, artists, educators, architects, landscape architects, conservationists, planners, investment advisers, and politicians, along with other professionals with real estate, direct mail, graphics, communications, and accounting skills in our mission. These people used their can do attitude and considerable skills to accomplish much more than one or two staff people could begin to cover. That trend continues to this day. PT's inclusive, trails-oriented mission—I call it the great common denominator—seems to attract a wide variety of interest and support. The fact that people are given distinct volunteer roles and achievable

LEFT: Peter Monro and Alix Hopkins made a pretty good team right from the start. **BELOW:** A ninety-foot crane swung the Fore River bridge into place.

Sometimes we had to live off the "whiff of a success," as I called it, for a year or more because of the notoriously long-term nature of these efforts.

responsibilities adds to the positive reputation of the organization as a worthwhile place to contribute scarce but appreciated time and energy.

The precedent for city trails was set in the mid-1980s when the Portland Parks and Recreation Department improved the Olmsted-designed, four-mile Baxter Boulevard (known locally as Back Cove) with a stone-dust path suitable for walking and biking. Conveniently, Back Cove served as the trail system hub, offering the first tangible proof that such amenities were popular and valuable assets. Portland Trails did not build the Back Cove trail, but we "borrowed" it for use as a hub for the entire thirty-mile network. Sometimes a little artistic license is necessary and appropriate.

We made a point of striving for distinct, tangible successes every year, and promoting them as such. Sometimes that goal proved challenging, as our projects ranged in size from a small stream bridge to a multimillion-dollar harborfront trail that redefined the eastern edge of the city and was emulated statewide, regionally, and nationally. Sometimes we had to live off the "whiff of a success," as I called it, for a year or more because of the notoriously long-term nature of these efforts. Yet to gather additional support, we had to give the *impression* of progress. Fortunately, as new trails opened, most people readily forgave the occasional gaps.

To get the word out I spoke at all hours of the day and night—to rotaries, scouts, corporate lunch crowds, divorce-counseling groups, women's literary societies. As I traveled around I learned to speak more comfortably before crowds, slowly transforming my early cinder-block-like demeanor. To raise our profile in a complementary sense I served on numerous local, regional, and statewide committees dealing with transportation, recreation, conservation, planning for development (also known as Smart Growth), and community quality-of-life issues. Our name and reputation began to grow as a result, as did our network of contacts.

A Small Package

In October of 1992, our first real project came in a small, acre-and-a-half package, containing Portland's only natural waterfall, subsequently named "Jewell Falls" after the donors, co-founder Tom Jewell's parents. On a beautiful fall day we held a dedication ceremony. More than seventy-five people attended, partly because I had spent much of the previous month promoting the waterfall with

members, neighbors, elected and city officials, and the press. Focused attention on public relations had begun in earnest.

Our next project involved raising money to build a 90-foot pedestrian bridge to the 85-acre Fore River Sanctuary, an urban wildlife preserve owned by the Maine Audubon Society. Accessible until then only by a small side road, it was unknown to most city residents. The bridge opened up, in essence, a new city park adjacent to a historic barge canal along the Fore River. During the three years required to raise money, obtain permits, and settle relations with concerned neighbors, project costs rose from an initial $40,000 to a staggering $140,000. In a stroke of good fortune, we received help in the form of a retired businessman who took over as volunteer project manager, handling construction and permitting details. It was tough going. At times we were not sure we would ever succeed. Working with a small committee composed of several board members, Maine Audubon staff, and the project manager, I learned to play cheerleader and friendly riot-act reader to keep things moving. I knew that as a fledgling organization, we simply *had* to make this happen to continue to demonstrate progress. And when a 200-foot-high crane swung the 90-foot bridge into place across the Fore River on a beautiful December day in 1994, with television cameras rolling, the grinding effort seemed fully worthwhile. Needless to say, we were exhausted; but we couldn't afford to slow down.

While working on the Fore River Bridge, Portland Trails simultaneously pursued several other projects. In an exemplary partnership encouraged by a former city councilor and business consultant, we worked with Maine based retailer L.L. Bean, the Horizon Foundation, the nonprofit Student Conservation Association, and the City of Portland to build the first section of a beautiful, wooded trail along the Stroudwater River. The Stroudwater, which

ABOVE: The Student Conservation Association's "front-country" crew in action. **ABOVE RIGHT:** Rotary Club volunteers shore up the Jewell Falls Bridge.

joins the Fore River, has a number of buildings dating from the eighteenth century along its banks. For four years prior to, and in preparation for, building the trail, several volunteers with professional skills helped out with conservation easement negotiation, permitting, and design. A developer donated the land along the river to the city as an open space corridor—a move that, in turn, aided him in obtaining future permits for his projects.

For several summers, student crews from the Student Conservation Association camped on-site, building trails, bridges, and boardwalks. A PT board member served as project coordinator the first year, and staff from the Portland Parks and Recreation Department provided construction and design expertise. Called a "front-country" project for its urban focus, this effort gave the participants a sense of pride gained from working together for a common purpose while exposed to sun, rain, and biting bugs. We later heard that the experience changed the course of several students' lives, shifting their educational focus to

environmental studies and regional planning. Such opportunities for gaining firsthand knowledge of the value of one's efforts are important—and all too rare. In recent years, the Stroudwater Trail has been extended upriver toward the neighboring town of Westbrook. It is my favorite Portland trail, among many good examples. Every fall, the brilliant red, yellow, and orange leaves reflect on the darkened river in a dazzling display of color and light. Anyone experiencing moments of serenity and connection with nature along this trail might never guess that downtown Portland is only minutes away.

Concurrently, we planned a new trail along the Fore River, linking Portland Harbor with the Eastern Prom Trail. Over five years the pieces fell into place, including a section along the historic twenty-mile Cumberland and Oxford Canal. Although the canal is no longer in use and is eroded in many places, the remaining towpath alongside offers a good surface for trails. This time we partnered with a private school and the Portland Parks and Recreation Department to design a route passing beautiful old trees along the riverbank and the former canal loading-dock site. PT received significant funding from a shipping company whose oil tanker had been involved in an oil spill that had fouled marshes in the Fore River several years earlier. To survey, design, and construct this section, we partnered with engineers, geologists, surveyors, and wetlands biologists from the local branch of a national environmental consulting firm. The firm recognized the value its expertise brought to Portland Trails, plus the positive public-relations benefits it received in return. We also received construction assistance from the Maine Conservation Corps. Together we built a series of boardwalks and observation platforms, and a mile of trail. It is important to note, however, that PT did not receive the actual damage award from the shipping company until two years after I had left—another example of how paralyzing the time lapse between vision and implementation can be without proper planning and perseverance. Nevertheless, today the trail continues reaching toward Portland Harbor, with the ultimate goal of circumnavigating the entire peninsula. Some of the pieces have been in play for five years or more; some await the right circumstances and timing to surface.

A Once-in-a-Century Opportunity

In the early 1990s, our flagship project unfolded at the foot of Munjoy Hill and the Eastern Promenade, resulting in a spectacular and historic two-mile, harbor-front park and trail. For several years, co-founder Nathan Smith and Eliza Cope Nolan, project manager from the Trust for Public Land (TPL), negotiated behind the scenes with railroad company Guilford Transportation Industries, and on behalf of the City of Portland and the Maine Department of Transportation, to acquire a thirty-acre, linear waterfront parcel. With stunning views of the islands in Casco Bay, this former rail yard almost became a marina and upscale housing complex during the economic boom of the 1980s. But the economic downturn and resulting project collapse in the early 1990s created a silver lining for Portland Trails, described by Bob Ganley, Portland's former city manager, as a "once-in-a-century opportunity." As Nathan recalls, "Eliza and I believed fully in the promise the acquisition held to revitalize this long-neglected and under-used section of the city."

Acting largely on faith, Eliza and Nathan spent countless hours persuading city and state officials of the project's merit. Simultaneously, we commissioned artistic renderings to interpret the vision for the new Eastern Promenade Trail and its potential value to the city. "The Trust for Public Land went far out on a limb by dedicating funds and staff time to support Eliza," Nathan says now, with immense gratitude, "all with absolutely no guarantee of success." Yet, somehow, everyone knew that this project represented significant possibilities—for the

city, for Portland Trails, for Maine, and for TPL.

The negotiations took several years and hundreds of hours of strategizing to play out. Juggling and accommodating so many players took a toll on our limited resources. Yet Nathan, Eliza, the board, and staff were dogged in their determination to succeed. Finally, in 1994 Nathan and Eliza prevailed when the Trust for Public Land obtained an option to purchase the Eastern Prom rail corridor, using $1.2 million in federal alternative transportation funding—the first, and still one of the largest such grants in Maine. A few months later, Portland Trails, TPL, and the city held a grand celebration in a tent at the edge of the bay, site of the future trail. Despite pouring rain and hungry mosquitoes, more than 250 people gathered to honor the occasion and the partners who made it happen.

Our next challenge was to engage the community in the trail planning process. As word leaked out, excitement and speculation grew. What would the trail look like? How would the landscape change? Who would use it? How safe would it be? How would the neighborhood change? All were important questions to investigate and answer. In response, the Portland City Council appointed a citizen committee to oversee the planning and design phases, drawing from a pool of individuals with an array of skills and perspectives. During the 1990s in Maine—a state resplendent with progressive thinkers—participation in public policy and public projects increased dramatically. Citizen input became the rule, serving to expand professional and civic networks. Tapping into this emerging tradition of grassroots activism, we found ourselves conducting our activities as though part of a populist political campaign.

The public review and planning process was long and painstaking. Working closely with Terrence J. DeWan & Associates (the landscape architecture firm previously responsible for giving form to the Shoreway Access Plan, subsequently chosen as the trail designers), the committee sorted its way through a series of aesthetic, engineering, and safety considerations. Occasionally PT and the city issued joint press releases, drumming up support and suggesting progress that was, quite frankly, difficult to sustain at times. When nothing tangible is evident, the public has only so much patience—a challenging scenario for us. We needed to get a section in place.

At the same time, an unanticipated backlash surfaced, coming from a few articulate, impassioned people wanting to preserve the raw, desolate, glass-strewn beauty of the former rail yard. On some level, the sentiment was well

The Mountain Division Trail

In 1994, another good opportunity arose when a rail company decided to abandon and subsequently sell a fifty-mile section of railroad with an average ninety-foot-wide right-of-way that ran from the New Hampshire border almost to Portland. The route passed through nine communities in Maine, but extended westward from New Hampshire through Vermont, and ultimately to Montreal, Canada. Since the 1980s, rails-with-trails (constructed next to train tracks, diverging when necessary for safety purposes) and rail trails (located directly on rail beds, after the tracks are removed) have become increasingly popular and cost-effective ways of revitalizing existing rail corridors. The Rails-to-Trails Conservancy is a national nonprofit organization dedicated to establishing both types of projects across the country (see Resources for more information). Immediately I felt compelled to see if enough common interest existed around creating a "rail-with-trail" on the Mountain Division line, and asked the Portland Trails board for their blessing to pursue that possibility. Citing the leadership role Portland Trails played in trail and alternative transportation issues and the trail's ultimate destination in Portland, the board agreed.

Subsequently we called a meeting of rail, trail, and economic development interests and determined the project had real merit for all three elements. Once again, a strong synergistic force was present; although the idea had been discussed in the past, the timing had not been right until just then. In response

we formed the Mountain Division Alliance, comprising twenty-six organizations, agencies, and individuals, and I became chair. On the collective strength of the assembled partners, the State of Maine acquired the section between Fryeburg in western Maine and Windham, about ten miles west of Portland. For nine years we worked closely with the Maine Department of Transportation and the Greater Portland Council of Governments (the regional planning agency) to conduct feasibility studies, engineering, and design, and to build public support before the first piece of trail was completed in 2003. Today the trail effort continues in both directions, buoyed by the construction of the initial four-mile section last year. Although the rail component of this project has languished, largely because of competing state budget priorities, the Alliance's vision to create a rail-with-trail remains undiminished.

understood. Things would change. The trail might not offer the same chances for solitary reflection. But we were convinced that the area would be safer, less littered, and offer a new connection to the city's waterfront. Opportunities for solitude would still exist, if one knew where and when to look.

Finally, in November of 1995 the first mile was constructed. As several of us watched excitedly from our second-floor office, huge earth-moving machines began carving a route along the water's edge. We promptly alerted the press, encouraging them to support the trail by reporting often on the construction activity. Almost immediately a remarkable thing happened: people started *using* the trail, barely waiting until the heavy equipment left. People of all sizes, ages, shapes, and athletic abilities showed up to see what all the hoopla was about. Small, noodle-legged boys on in-line skates showed up with their families, and hard-core runners flew by in packs during lunchtime every day. Wheelchair users came, as did mothers with strollers, and mere meanderers. There was

BELOW: Plotting the next move.

People greeted each other in passing as if meeting on a woodland trail—somewhat unusual in an urban setting, where anonymity is more the norm.

something here for everyone. It was a wonderful sight. We knew we had hit a home run.

Completing the first mile of the Eastern Prom Trail brought PT significant gains in credibility, community pride, and connectivity to the waterfront in ways not apparent before. People greeted each other in passing as if meeting on a woodland trail—somewhat unusual in an urban setting, where anonymity is more the norm. Six months later, in the spring of 1996, the second half of the Eastern Prom Trail was constructed. And in 2000, the final link was made under Tukey's Bridge, between Back Cove and the Eastern Prom Trail. With over six miles of off-road, shorefront trail added to the network, a major portion of PT's goal was in place. Now, each June the intoxicating scent of *Rosa rugosa* blossoms drifts across the trail. From there, visitors can watch ships entering the harbor and the ever-changing light reflecting on the islands across the bay.

Partners

Partnerships were the cornerstones of Portland Trails' success. In a key move early on, co-founder Dick Spencer procured a National Park Service Rivers & Trails technical assistance grant (see Resources) to help the infant organization along. Charlie Tracy, the Rivers & Trails project manager, brought with him numerous community organizing and communications skills. Under his guidance, and with help from Portland's planning, recreation, and urban development staff, PT printed a colorful vision map of the proposed trail system. We also designed a distinctive logo, with an instantly recognizable view of the city skyline across the water from Back Cove. The purpose of both pieces was to help persuade officials, corporate leaders, foundations, and the public to embrace our goal of a thirty-mile trail network. The map worked well as a visual tool because people could locate their homes or offices and where a nearby trail might pass. No longer would they need to drive to take a decent hike; they could do so easily within city limits. Dick Spencer claims, "The minute I saw that vision map, I knew that we had it. Our map redefined the city."

Our close working relationship with the City of Portland, particularly with the Planning and Urban Development, Parks and Recreation, and Public Works Departments, was critical. In many ways, our collaborative methods changed the ways in which Portland's citizens groups interacted with and advised municipal officials. From the start, each department gave financial, in-kind, planning, and

"The minute I saw that vision map, I knew that we had it. Our map redefined the city."

moral support to Portland Trails, and many staffers became individual members. One invaluable asset, among many, was Rick Knowland, who served as liaison between the city planning department and PT. Knowland alerted us when projects of potential interest arose. Portland Trails also enjoyed strong backers on the city council, including current U.S. congressman Tom Allen, a former councilor who spearheaded a citywide transportation plan during the early 1990s that featured trails.

Also during the 1990s, the Maine Department of Conservation broadened its focus on trails and public access beyond the more traditional hunting and fishing uses. State parks, especially those in southern Maine, had experienced exponential increases in visitation, and trail acquisition and improvement funds became available through state and federal sources.

Maine's large and active land trust community lent moral support, expertise, and credibility. In particular we benefited from our relationship with the respected Maine Coast Heritage Trust, which provided technical knowledge and review for a conservation easement along the Stroudwater Trail. These relationships were mutually beneficial. Portland Trails became increasingly prominent nationally for its strong leadership, collaboration, distinctive graphics, concerted effort at public relations, and high level of community involvement, and our success informed the work of many Maine land trusts that adapted our tactics for their own use. In turn, land trusts became more inclined to consider the broad-ranging benefits of conducting their work in a community-based manner, increasing their use of trails and public access as helpful and effective public-relations tools.

The Maine Department of Transportation (MDOT) also became a significant partner as transportation evolved to incorporate more than just highways and bridges. An entire culture changed as transportation became viewed as increasingly integral to the quality of community life. Alternatives such as rail, bus, bicycle, and pedestrian access became part of the mix. Citizen input seriously challenged the old thinking of longtime transportation officials, who ultimately rose to the occasion to embrace the change. From its inception, Portland Trails embodied this new way of thinking and helped to convince state officials that they could work with knowledgeable and dedicated citizen activists.

In its most substantial contribution, MDOT worked with Portland Trails to procure federal alternative transportation funding for the Eastern Prom Trail

RIGHT: Dick Spencer, PT's co-founder extraordinaire.

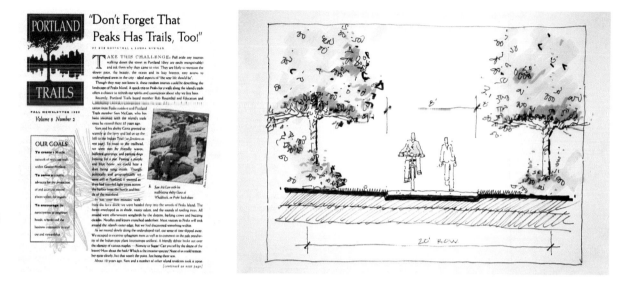

through ISTEA (Intermodal Surface Transportation Efficiency Act, mandated in 1991), to the tune of $1.2 million. The trail project was literally a groundbreaking effort in Maine, requiring a leap of faith from many people to ensure proper planning, funding, and construction.

Making the Case

To reach a wider audience, Portland Trails began to promote the multidimensional benefits of trails and highlight the links among economic and community development, transportation, recreation, public health, and spiritual well-being. A "Case for Support" publication encouraged corporations, foundations, elected officials, and the public to invest time and money. We also designed a punchy, informative, and graphically distinctive newsletter to establish a professional reputation. As I often say, "We have only one chance to make a good first impression." By highlighting people with diverse interests, the newsletter conveyed our growing sense of momentum, progress, and public support. These communications tactics worked well, as during those first few years people regularly perceived Portland Trails as having a staff of five or more. What we really had was an active board, a deep pool of volunteers, and one, later two and then three, energetic staff members.

Every year the PT Communications Committee enjoyed brainstorming ideas for our annual appeal, along with ways of harnessing the talent of Portland's vibrant arts community. A combination of professional photographs, original art, and witty phrasing gave Portland Trails our unique look. Artists mostly donated their services, and the results were almost always well received. The committee felt that showcasing a variety of artistic interpretations was important in engaging additional constituents.

Portland Trails consistently attracted a broad array of volunteers, both in number and in skills. During the first decade, turnover occurred normally, even liberally, but the organization rarely lost a beat. As our momentum increased, so too did the workload. By the mid-1990s, help was sorely needed. Until then we had managed well with the help of one volunteer who upgraded our membership database from the file-card era to the computer. But as we added members through a series of direct-mail solicitations, we found it necessary to add staff in membership services. As a result, Portland Trails grew from fifty to 650 members.

Giving Something Back

As we achieved success, Portland Trails recognized the importance of reaching out to the next generation of citizens and trail stewards. In essence, we possessed a blank canvas for creating an innovative environmental education program, with room to include new partners as opportunities arose. With this came the need to hire staff with an educational orientation. Jessica Burton came from the Chewonki Foundation, an experiential environmental education center and camp based in Wiscasset, Maine (see Resources). Portland Trails gave her the latitude to create an integrated program, using trails as outdoor classrooms. In response she brought people from the art museum, historic preservation organization, transit district, regional planning agency, a state conservation agency, and other environmental education programs on board as a working advisory committee.

View of Baxter Boulevard,. Portland, Maine — D-21

She recruited teachers to help design a flexible, fun, and usable curriculum. For example, classes worked on aspects of trail making—including negotiating with landowners for access, planning and design, permitting, construction, signage, and, of course, celebration. Because some students had not spent much time in nature, this experience was a new adventure for them. They learned firsthand the value of perseverance, creativity, and communication, while making lasting contributions in their neighborhoods. They also learned about creating a sense of community—both how and why it is important to do so. Jess also created a multiday teacher workshop to promote the ties that trails engender with other social, cultural, economic, and cultural organizations and agencies.

Laura Newman, our second education coordinator, brought an eclectic background of teaching English and art. When it became evident that PT needed to reach people of all ages, outreach was added to her job. Laura soon enlisted the utility company, health-care and wellness providers, and social service agencies, and added a focus on program diversity. She developed a model whereby classes created trails from their schools to parks, other schools, or social centers such as libraries. The project proved so popular that Portland Trails consistently receives requests for assistance at other schools in Portland and beyond. Current plans include forming a greater Portland "Schoolground Greening Coalition," through public-private partnerships.

Despite its continued successes, Portland Trails, like all nonprofits, occasionally experienced traumatic and debilitating moments. One such incident occurred during the redesign of the historic, Olmsted-designed Baxter Boulevard, the road that circled Back Cove. As the popular 3.5-mile stone-dust loop around the cove began to receive greater use, concern spread about safety for bikers, runners, and walkers, and particularly for young children. In response, the city council appointed a committee of interested stakeholders to study and recommend options for improvements. The resulting process had the effect of polarizing the community, pitting Portland Trails against historic preservationists in an oversimplified battle between safety and aesthetics. Lines were drawn firmly between maintaining the boulevard's historic design integrity and offering appropriate buffers and barriers to keep bicyclists and pedestrians separated from moving traffic. Particularly challenging was the fact that many "opponents" of the safety barriers were generally ardent PT supporters. The ordeal played out in the media. Tempers ran hot. In the furor, we lost several key supporters. Some returned to the fold because of solid relationships that transcended the conflict, but it was an especially difficult time. The hard lesson we

learned was to conduct delicate, controversial work within the committee, not in public—especially when so much was at stake.

The situation was resolved temporarily but will need revisiting in the next few years. Next time, one hopes, both the process and the outcome will be different. For me personally, this conflict was the most difficult of my tenure. As a collaboratively oriented person, I worried that much time and effort spent building relationships might be simply swept away over one incendiary issue. Fortunately, that very emphasis on connection was what saved us from costly alienation.

Relinquishing the Balloons

After more than seven and a half years at the helm, the time came for me to step away from Portland Trails. This move was not because of lack of enthusiasm, but rather, exhaustion. I often likened my job to having the responsibility for keeping at least forty day-old helium balloons—all hovering precariously near the ground—in the air by moving back and forth among them and bumping them skyward in turn. Clearly this was a good move both for the organization and for me. I gave the board six months' notice, allowing ample time to determine successive leadership needs. The Portland Trails board then created a strategic search process based on moving their priorities forward, enabling them to find the

right person to carry out their vision. The board showed real leadership during a challenging time for any organization, when the baton passes from founding executive director to successor.

The board found the right person in Nan Cumming, a longtime Portland Trails member, formerly with the Maine Historical Society. She brought many years of nonprofit experience, particularly in programs, grants, and fund-raising. In Nan, the board found the perfect complement to all that had gone into building the organization. For her part, Nan loves her job as much as I did. "Being director of Portland Trails is the best job ever," she says. "Even if it takes us years of planning and fund-raising to develop a project, A job well done is so evident. . . . In the end the trail is right out there in front of you."

As time grew short before my departure, I was determined to honor our journey thus far. Although it was billed as a farewell party, the large gathering of volunteers, staff, members, and sponsors gave everyone the chance to celebrate our success together, and to look ahead to new opportunities. In my final newsletter editorial, I wrote:

> Who would have thought that a fledgling urban land trust would grow to
> incorporate so many elements—land conservation, alternative transportation,

recreation, public health and well-being, environmental education, and community and economic development? How did this happen? It happened because a great idea, hatched through collaboration, attracted a vital and committed group of people to foster it. And the interest and enthusiasm of these volunteers has not wavered in all that time. The most wonderful people keep walking in our door with something to contribute. One of Portland Trails' greatest accomplishments is that we helped people to see the relevance of land conservation to their everyday lives. The trails are just up the street, or around the corner. They connect neighborhoods, parks, schools, and businesses, representing a significant part of Portland's community fabric.

I had been given the gift of working with an organization almost from inception, and then the chance to feel the enormous surge as we struck a responsive chord in all sections of the city and across the state. And the experience changed the lives of most of us in many positive ways. Although titles have changed and many people have moved on, their contributions endure. In the process they learned about their skills, gained friends, and became respected community leaders in their own right. Dick Spencer went on to found Rangeley Lakes Heritage Trust, one of Maine's preeminent land trusts. He practices land use, school, and public finance law, and lends environmental policy expertise as a board member of several nonprofit organizations. Tom Jewell specializes in real estate law and continues to play a major role in developing new Portland trails to add to the network. Nathan Smith and former board president Jim Cohen currently sit on the Portland City Council, concentrating on housing, transportation, community development, and open space issues. And as this story was finished, Nathan was elected mayor of Portland. Other volunteers over the past decade have engaged in local and state government; local, regional, and national politics; business, education, civic, and nonprofit endeavors—all benefiting people in communities across the state and the region.

As for me, my experience in guiding the organization toward its full potential revealed and affirmed my innate abilities. Portland Trails became a catalyst for my subsequent work on other trail, conservation, and community collaboration projects. These days I serve mostly on lean but effective nonprofit boards, and seek to help people in communities around the country and internationally get started on their own good projects. In short, ours was the ride of a lifetime. And we are not done yet.

"A source of hope in a world that feels pretty desperate right now."

—Ann Gilbert, farm member

2

Common Harvest Farm

Osceola, Wisconsin—*A collaboration of farm owners, farm members, and a regional land conservation organization saves land, produces healthy food, and supports a small family farm in the Midwest.*

This is a story about relationship and shared values, using "community-supported agriculture" (CSA) as the framework. In the CSA model, "members" purchase shares of produce from a farm during the growing season every year. In so doing, they eat healthy and locally grown food while also supporting a family farm. What impressed me most about the owners and members of Common Harvest Farm was their thoughtful and collective commitment to the values of simplicity, sharing, and sustainability. Some people in this story came to embrace the CSA concept through faith-based inspiration acquired from teachings and discussions at their churches. Others arrived through their philosophical beliefs in living and eating close to the land. Whatever the source, the connections here run strong and deep all around.

As you approach Common Harvest Farm in western Wisconsin, your eye is first drawn to the large red barn with a poem by William Carlos Williams painted on the front in white lettering. It reads:

so much depends
upon
a red wheel
barrow
glazed with rain
water
beside the white
chickens.

Not a wheelbarrow, but an old pickup—a sentinel of sorts—greets visitors. Looking as if it has seen better days it is, nevertheless, a comforting sight—as if it has withstood years of changing weather conditions and seasonal cycles with true grace. The white farmhouse sits on a rise overlooking the fields and other outbuildings. Several workhorses graze off in a distant field. Below the house, where the pond has recently overflowed its banks, the farm children—Annie, Grace, and William—splash happily in the mud. It's been a wet spring and there is also standing water in some fields.

Dan Guenther and Margaret Pennings, a husband-and-wife team, are Common Harvest Farm's co-owners. Together they've long held a vision to nurture communities with organic, locally produced food through community-supported agriculture. With the 1997 purchase of this forty-acre farm in Osceola, Wisconsin (about an hour away from the "Twin Cities" of Minneapolis and St. Paul, Minnesota), they've set out to realize their dream. Many other people

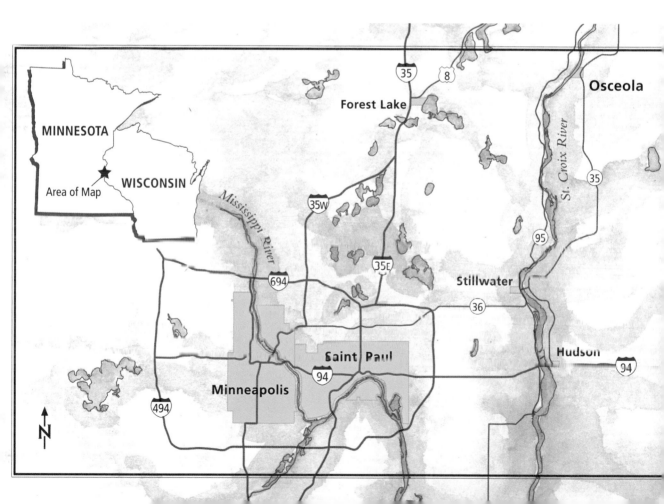

The Red Wheelbarrow

so much depends
upon

a red wheel
barrow

glazed with rain
water

beside the white
chickens

William Carlos Williams

on their journey were to help them hone and articulate their vision. And they were to discover, in Margaret's words, "When you start working closer to the land, something spiritual is going to happen."

Margaret and Dan met at Holden Village, an ecumenical Christian retreat center rooted in the Lutheran tradition, in the Cascade Mountains of Washington during the 1980s. Holden Village challenged participants (who volunteered there, often for several years) to focus on "simple living, simple food, and eating lower on the food chain," as well as on peace and social justice. When the couple moved back to Minneapolis, they joined the Community of St. Martin, a church established around many similar concerns. Here they began to learn about community-supported agriculture, a unique model of local agriculture whose roots reach back thirty years.

According to the Robyn Van En Center for Community-Supported Agriculture in Chambersburg, Pennsylvania, the concept got its start when a group of women in Japan, who were concerned about the increase in food imports and the corresponding decrease in the farming population, initiated a direct growing and purchasing relationship with local farms. This arrangement, called *teikei* in Japanese, translates to "putting the farmers' face on food." This idea soon caught on, traveled to Europe, and was later adapted to the U.S., where it was given the name "community-supported agriculture" in 1985 at Indian Line Farm in Massachusetts. By March 2004, more than 1,100 CSA farms existed across the U.S. and Canada, and the number keeps growing.

Community-supported agriculture, a partnership between a farm and a community of supporters, provides a direct link between the production and consumption of food. Supporters cover a farm's yearly operating budget by purchasing seasonal harvest shares. CSA members commit to supporting the farm during the growing season and assume the costs, risks, and bounty of growing food along with the farmer. Members help pay for seeds, fertilizer,

water, equipment maintenance, labor, and other costs. In return, the farm provides, to the best of its ability, a healthy supply of seasonal fresh produce. This process results in a responsible relationship between people and their food—a partnership that includes the land on which food is grown and those who grow it, helping to create an economically stable farm operation. In return, farmers and growers are guaranteed a reliable market for a diverse selection of crops.

As the Robyn Van En Center also suggests, CSA encourages communication and cooperation among area farmers and guarantees a market for their produce. It supports the biodiversity of a given area and the diversity of agriculture by preserving small farms producing a wide variety of crops. CSA creates opportunity for dialogue between local farmers and consumers, creates a sense of social responsibility and stewardship of local land, develops a regional food supply and strong local economy, and honors the knowledge and experience of growers and producers working with small to medium farms. (For more information, see Resources.)

"When the concept of CSA began in the 1980s in this country," Margaret Pennings says, "Dan and I were in the right place at the right time. As we began to read about CSAs, we realized we already worked and lived this way at Holden Village, a community where people make conscious choices about their lifestyle by understanding their connection to the rest of creation." For her, faith is at the heart of it all, "exploring our connection to others, to God, and to the Earth." For Dan it is perhaps more a question of reconnecting with farming. "Our food system has become very impersonal and institutionalized," he says, "Most people's experience with food is in the checkout line. We've lost the culture of agriculture."

"A Wonderful Sense of Dependency"

Margaret and Dan began their quest by holding meetings in their Minneapolis neighborhood of Seward, talking about food and how things had changed since their childhood. "These early meetings were instructive, but mostly we just listened," Dan says. With the support of friends and community, Dan and Margaret leased land in the western suburbs of Minneapolis. They raised vegetables to supply St. Martin's Table, a nonprofit restaurant and bookstore. The restaurant's simple vegetarian menu includes homemade soups and bread. Servers are volunteers, and profits go toward hunger projects. Unfortunately, during this time Dan and Margaret's leased farmland was sold for development. Back then they couldn't afford to buy land, but they found it difficult to continue to work on rented land because of the uncertain tenure, and the time and money it took to make the soil more productive.

Thus, after eight years and two more moves, Dan and Margaret knew they needed their own farm. With the encouragement of friends, they began looking in western Wisconsin, about an hour northeast of Minneapolis. They found a good prospect located on fertile land along the St. Croix River, which forms the boundary between Wisconsin and Minnesota. But as is often the case with small entrepreneurs, the asking price for the farm was clearly out of their reach. Undaunted, they began to search for creative ways of funding their vision, including

What is Community-Supported Agriculture and How Does It Work?

Food is a basic human need. Yet for most of us, it is merely an inexpensive commodity that we take for granted. How, where, and by whom our food is grown are generally not topics of conversation around the dinner table. Considering the current situation in agriculture, perhaps they should be. Food in the U.S. travels an average of 1,300 miles from the farm to the market shelf. Almost every state in the U.S. buys 85 to 90 percent of its food from farms outside of its borders. In Massachusetts, for example, this food import imbalance translates to a $4 billion leak in the state economy on an annual basis. University of Massachusetts studies have determined that the state could produce closer to 35 percent of its food supply. Further, this 20-percent increase would contribute $1 billion annually to

the state's economy. Increased local food production would add considerably to the economies of many other states.

Meanwhile, the nation's best farmland is being lost to commercial and residential development at an accelerating rate. At the same time, retiring older farmers, increasing land and production costs, low food prices, competing land uses, the lack of incentive for young people to enter farming, and the fundamental restructuring of the national and global economy all combine to make farming and local food production in the U.S. an increasingly difficult task. Community-supported agriculture represents a viable alternative to the prevailing situation and gives consumers a direct relationship with the food they eat. —*The Robyn Van En Center for Community-Supported Agriculture*

speaking with the former executive director of the Wisconsin Farmland Conservancy, Tom Quinn. Quinn came up with the idea of exchanging a conservation easement (relinquishing future development rights) for shares in the farm's equity, having witnessed similar transactions taking place successfully in small communities in Germany. Impressed by Dan's and Margaret's vision and commitment both to conservation and the community, he and his board were willing to foster this potentially mutually beneficial process. Dan and Margaret concurred, appealing to their former CSA members, their church group in Minneapolis, and the Conservancy for financial assistance in buying the farm. The response was overwhelming.

As a result, a mix of mechanisms provided the up-front capital necessary to purchase the farm at a lower interest rate. Nearly seventy people from their CSA (remarkably, as Margaret tells it, almost 50 percent of their members), plus other church and Conservancy members helped Dan and Margaret by making cash donations to the nonprofit Wisconsin Farmland Conservancy, now called the West Wisconsin Land Trust (WWLT). Ten members invested in seven-year produce shares as their method of contributing to the total figure. The remaining 50 percent of the money came from family sources. The income was pooled and used to purchase a conservation easement from Dan and Margaret in 1997, helping them to afford the land and make capital improvements. In return for an easement on the farm, the land trust purchased a share of the equity in the farm operation. In its current role, WWLT helps oversee the upgrading of the farm, buildings, and equipment. At the time, this example was somewhat rare because CSA was still a fairly new concept. Today, having proved itself as a viable solution to inadequate funding, it is used more commonly.

Many CSA members donated in-kind services such as labor and building materials for the farmhouse, made one-time financial contributions, and purchased seven-year produce shares. Dan acknowledges that the local bank took a big risk on a first-time mortgage—especially considering the restrictions of a conservation easement, conceivably reducing the overall land value. Quite simply, as Dan claims, Common Harvest Farm could not have come into being without the moral and financial support of so many people. For these and other reasons, Dan and Margaret feel particularly strong bonds with their members. "We have a wonderful sense of dependency. As we box the vegetables each week, we always think about the people receiving them," Margaret acknowledges.

Coming Together

Common Harvest Farm doesn't need to advertise for new members—it's all word of mouth, and every year there's a waiting list. It offers 220 shares, serving

"Just knowing about other members gives me hope that people are out there doing good work, and that things really can change."

OPEN SPACES

Preserving Critical Wetlands in Polk County

PRESERVING WESTERN WISCONSIN'S NATURAL CHARACTER

ABOVE. WWLT was instrumental in helping Dan and Margaret purchase the farm through donations to acquire the land and place conservation restrictions on it.
RIGHT: Mindy Ahlers-Olmstead and Kraig Olmstead are newer, but no less enthusiastic, farm members.

about four hundred families from nine acres of vegetable production. Because the produce usually is plentiful, most members divide their weekly share with friends or neighbors, a practice that is heartily recommended to encourage greater community connections.

Members receive a renewal letter and contract—a "Statement of Expectations"—to clarify their roles annually. Although many members intend to visit or help out, in reality, most don't. But the other intangible benefits for members include relationships with kindred spirits, increased knowledge, and substantial personal growth resulting from the collective efforts of farmers and members in support of Common Harvest Farm. Several farm members shared their thoughts on these benefits with me.

Ann Gilbert and Dan Pederson live with their son David in a quiet, tree-lined neighborhood in Minneapolis. Dan is a freelance librarian; Ann is the registrar for an adult education program focusing on English as a second language. Ann and Dan don't remember exactly how their connections with CSAs began long ago—probably through neighborhood friends or their church, the Community of St. Martin. For Dan, being part of Common Harvest Farm—though it is an hour away—has made him feel more grounded in his own neighborhood. He and Ann split their share of produce each week with neighbors. Ann considers the weekly produce pickup a treasured summer ritual, which she performs by pulling her small red wagon over to the drop site, often accompanied by her son.

Dan and Ann look forward to their time at the farm. To them it is a place of solace when they need to get away from their urban environment. Dan and Ann help out at the farm, planting vegetables and later taking pride in the harvest. For Dan, the experience has helped him to reconnect to his early days on a family farm in Minnesota. Ann loves to be out by herself in the field, weeding carrots, or at harvest time—for her, a highly meditative and restorative practice. "It is such rolling, beautiful land," she exclaims.

"When Dan and Margaret made their home at Common Harvest Farm, there was a real feeling of celebration," Ann notes. Dan Pederson adds, "Owning the land seemed to bring a different sense of commitment, as did building the soil

over a period of years and fostering the notion of stewardship." Citing an example, they mention the annual Harvest Festival, which builds a heightened sense of community and support for CSA by bringing everyone involved together to celebrate another growing season. "The relationships formed here are really important," Ann says. "I gain so much more than just vegetables." Every morning at home in Minneapolis, she wakes up and checks out the weather, thinking about its effect on the farm. As members, Dan adds, they share in both loss and abundance. And they've learned to relate to farming in a new way, with greater empathy for the challenges small farms must face in order to survive. As Ann says, "Dan and Margaret have a whole community behind them. We buy shares because it matters to us that the farm succeeds. And CSAs help keep farms viable."

To Ann, Common Harvest Farm is her "source of hope in a world that feels desperate right now. In my small way, I make a concrete difference by participating—and by choosing another possibility." She has acquired a broadened

sense of choices for living in relationship to the land, in direct contrast with the pace of events occurring in the twenty-first century, where globalization, conflict, and instant technology are commonplace. "Since 9/11," Dan Pederson observes, "people are seeking and nesting more at a local level. People are aware of how much we are trashing the environment, but they can't really get a handle on the notion of global warming. They can, however, understand it on a micro scale, as exemplified by the farm." In Ann's words, "There would be a big hole in the fabric of our lives if we were not part of Common Harvest Farm."

Other members include Kraig Olmstead and Mindy Ahlers-Olmstead, a young couple who joined Common Harvest Farm three years ago. In their former lives she was a corporate consultant and he, a computer programmer. Mindy now works at an international crafts import store, and Kraig is a musician. Kraig and Mindy like to eat local, seasonal foods—to them, a more sustainable way to live. Although Kraig and Mindy understand that an open invitation exists to help on the farm, they have not yet participated. They do, however, enjoy meeting people at the weekly drop site. For Mindy, "Just knowing about other members gives me hope that people are out there doing good work, and that things really can change."

Janet Anderson is a young mother and drop-site coordinator. She learned about the CSA concept from her participation at Holden Village, the retreat community in Washington State where Dan and Margaret met. In her role of hosting the weekly produce distribution, Janet is a keen observer. People bring their own bags, allocating and transferring the food and recycling the boxes for next time. Janet usually disappears after the initial setup, letting people fend for themselves using the honor system. She notes with interest how members get to know each other better, "like people on a regular bus route. They are polite at first, warming up and soon looking forward to seeing each other both here and elsewhere." As she suggests, "Every neighborhood should have an opportunity like this. It is so important to encourage this where you live."

Amy Middleton is an environmental planner who runs a consulting business with two other women. After living in various cities, about six years ago she and her partner moved out to a rural setting in Dresser, a few towns away from Common Harvest Farm. With a career and a young daughter in tow, she had little time to garden herself and appreciated the opportunity to buy produce from the farm. Knowing also how hard Dan and Margaret work, she wanted to support them in their efforts.

Amy is involved in the nearby Standing Cedars Community Land Conservancy,

and seeks to encourage landowners to protect their land. Standing Cedars was formed in 1994 by the former Wisconsin Farmland Conservancy in response to growing concern about disappearing farmland and natural areas and the desire to help preserve a five mile stretch along the St. Croix River. Her business, MMC Associates, has created educational and promotional materials for several Conservancy projects. Amy plans to place an easement on her forty acres to set an example that, she hopes, will encourage four neighboring families to join her in protecting their land. Such a collective effort would create a large contiguous area, with greater ecological value as wildlife habitat and open space than one smaller parcel would offer by itself.

Making it Work: "We Just let the boxes do the talking"

To build support for land conservation, Amy Middleton says, Standing Cedars representatives speak proactively with groups of farmers about the benefits of placing easements on agricultural land. When such a conservation agreement occurs, the land stays open and the farmers often receive much-needed monetary compensation. Arousing their interest eases the way for preserving more open space and therefore helping to maintain a viable agricultural economy in the valley where Common Harvest Farm is located. Everybody wins.

Amy respects the collective commitments and risks undertaken by both farmers and members. She also likes to discover other members in her travels between Osceola and Minneapolis/St. Paul. Her support of CSAs may well stem from being raised by parents who had cherry orchards in Michigan. She grew up farming and understands well the challenges faced by farmers.

Jo Anne Rohricht lives with her husband in one of St. Paul's more stately neighborhoods, lined with big, old trees. Holding a master's degree in theological studies, she is now retired. Jo Anne has been involved in several worthwhile endeavors, including the Block Nurse Program—a community effort caring for the elderly in their own neighborhoods. She's also engaged in the Land Stewardship Project, which encourages good stewardship in agriculture (in her words, "caring for the land and the people making their livings on it") and helps farmers and their farms to become environmentally and economically sustainable. After joining the Land Stewardship board as a self-described "urban consumer activist," she now chairs it.

Jo Anne and her husband started with another CSA, coming to Common Harvest Farm after the first one folded. When a prior drop-site coordinator in her neighborhood moved away, she took over the duties. Jo Anne likes the fact that both CSA and the Land Stewardship Project embody the universal themes

of "land governed and cared for by many people—a real economic democracy."
She also recognizes that since "Margaret and Dan are working against the grain,
they inspire the rest of us. Some things have to change from the bottom up. You
have to keep on working for something that you know is right, even though
you can't yet see through to the other side." To Jo Anne, such tangible and
meaningful examples as Common Harvest Farm show that people can make
a difference. Through her activism she's learned that, "We have allies and they
are legion—people sharing beliefs even though they may be across the country
from one another."

According to Margaret and Dan, success for a CSA is determined by a high
membership return rate. In their case, more than one hundred members out
of 220 have stayed with them for more than ten years. Although they keep in
touch by periodically placing notes in the members' delivery boxes, they know
they could do a better job of communicating. But their time is seriously limited.
"At this point," Margaret notes, "we just let the boxes do the talking," through
the quality and variety of produce.

To complement their selections, Margaret and Dan offer a "dairy share" to
members, connecting them to farmers in southeastern Minnesota for butter,
cheese, and other products, as well as to other area farmers. When appropriate,
they recommend farmers' markets—particularly those with an emphasis on selling locally grown food. They promote "coffee shares" with the Fair Trade philosophy of buying shade-grown coffee and giving "fair" prices to growers. Such
products often accompany the weekly deliveries and serve to round out the
range of healthy products available. This exchange benefits all sides by creating a
larger customer base for every enterprise.

Each fall, the farm hosts a potluck Harvest Festival. The popular event features
farm tours, where Dan is likely to "wax eloquent" about vegetables (especially
his kale), the land, and the triumphs and challenges of the past season. For many,

a particularly memorable scene each year is the pumpkin-lined walkway along the entrance to the farm. Activities have included a bonfire, music, an art show, and always lots of children running around. A sense of abundance and gratitude for another good year prevails.

The farm employs several summer interns, and recruits high school laborers and volunteer help from members. Last summer David Bauer, a young man from Milwaukee and recent University of Minnesota graduate with a degree in history, worked as an intern. Bauer's prior experience came from growing food in urban backyards. Not long ago, his grandfather announced his interest in passing the family farm along to an heir. David figured that spending time working at Common Harvest was a good way to learn the skills and parameters of organic farming and—he hopes—to help him decide whether or not to take on the big responsibility of his grandfather's farm.

In thinking about the future lately, Dan and Margaret have considered offering the farm as a place of retreat. In that vein, they are leaning toward creating a quiet space—perhaps a cabin near the pond—for winter use by people wishing to write or reflect in a tranquil and beautiful setting. Dan has connected with

Kohlrabi

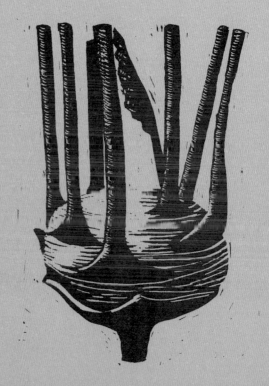

Margaret Pennings tells an amusing story about a farm member who called her one summer in great confusion. He wondered what a vegetable looking rather like "an alien creature" was doing in his box. It was a greenish plant with tube-like appendages sticking out of it. He was truly mystified, having never before seen anything quite like it. From his description, and without missing a beat, Margaret knew it was a kohlrabi, a member of the mustard family, also called a turnip cabbage. She suggested he purchase a cookbook called *From Asparagus to Zucchini: A Guide to Farm-Fresh Seasonal Produce*, published by the Madison Area Community-Supported Agriculture Coalition (see Resources), which could help him out by suggesting recipes for cooking and eating the strange thing.

some nearby Amish farmers, from whom he has learned a great deal. The farm now has five workhorses, and Dan has partnered with the Amish to design a variety of farm tools that are, as he calls it, "gentle on the land." The big red barn will need to be rebuilt soon because of deterioration (due, somewhat surprisingly, to the absence of animals in it for many years—according to Margaret, the breath and body heat of farm animals kept the interior of the barn from freezing, and once they were gone the constant freezing and thawing cycles took their toll on the structure). In the next few years Margaret and Dan may engage an Amish couple to build the frame and afterward invite the farm community to help raise a new barn.

Building Community

To Dan and Margaret, the food they grow strengthens existing communities, offering food as another unifying resource. As Margaret says, "Our food incubates the threads of courage and creativity that exist in every life." These threads then begin to intersect with other elements, creating larger, more wonderful possibilities in the world. "We live in times where people really want to be part of positive change," Dan feels. Quoting Gandhi, he adds, "So we are going to make the road as we go." Translated to Common Harvest Farm as Dan interprets it: "We are laying the stones as we walk, and we are all doing it together." This sentiment is best exemplified by the collaborative transaction that enabled Dan and Margaret to purchase the farm, creating a classic win-win scenario by permanently relinquishing the farm's future development rights while offering income tax deductions to the donors. Further, the effort introduced the CSA and church members to the work of the West Wisconsin Land Trust, and the land trust members to CSA.

Yet, as current WWLT executive director Rick Gauger describes their actions, it is important to remember also that "Dan and Margaret showed an exemplary

level of commitment to the land and the community. We don't often run into individuals with such vision and determination. All in all, this was a perfect partnership a great model of synergy between the farmers, the community, and the land trust. And it's a nice way to achieve greater community involvement."

These benefits extended even further, Rick says, when a number of individuals who made gifts toward the farm later purchased adjacent land, placed easements on it, and gave Dan and Margaret first right of refusal. The Standing Cedars Community Land Conservancy now holds 1,100 neighboring acres under conservation easement, creating a sizable protected area that includes Common Harvest Farm. And nearby farmers who witnessed the success of this project became inspired to place easements on their own land. In Rick's opinion, the project also showed how well farming and conservation can coexist, in this case, by using organic methods—something even the most rabid environmentalists can embrace while continuing to resist other, more chemically dependent farming practices.

Reaching a Wider Audience

Through the innovative solution that helped them to realize their passionate vision, Dan and Margaret—and the farm and land trust members—took the concept of collective action a significant step further. What began as a traditional CSA project expanded in scope to resolve a significant financial challenge by investing, quite literally, in the ground. As an added benefit, their project promoted land conservation as a community-preservation tool to a wider audience. By combining resources to acquire the land and purchase the development rights to the farm, these supporters ensured its permanent protection, along with the well-being of the farm family and that of the community it fed.

Recently Margaret reported that last spring, they took down the old red barn with the help of their Amish neighbors, retaining 70 percent of the original post-and-beam structure. A few weeks ago, more than three hundred people—many of them farm members—gathered over a two-day period to participate in a barn raising. According to Margaret, those involved were thoroughly engaged in the process. One woman who participated exclaimed about the large amount of work done in a relatively short time, noting, "It's just amazing what people can do when given an opportunity."

And, by the way, when asked about the fate of the Red Wheelbarrow poem painted on the old barn wall, Margaret reassured me that it too was saved. The panel will be reattached to the front of the new barn, to continue to greet visitors and members alike with its distinct and thoughtful message.

"No one would dream of tearing down the cathedrals of Europe; how could anyone

even think of cutting down these trees?" —Kelsey Jack, age fourteen

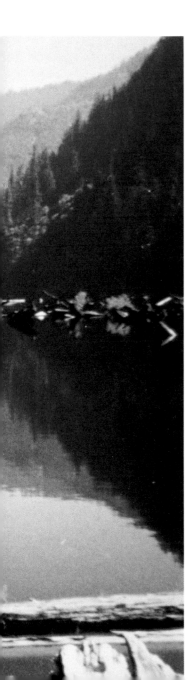

3

Canyon Lake Creek Community Forest

Bellingham, Washington—*A local land trust, county government, several timber companies, a private foundation, and a university, with guidance from the state chapter of a national conservation organization, mount an unusual campaign to save ancient trees in the Pacific Northwest.*

This is a story about daring, where visionaries from a small land trust in Bellingham, Washington, formed critical partnerships and pulled out all the stops to preserve an ancient forest about to be sold for logging. When I visited the people involved in this project, I was struck by how fully they embodied the qualities necessary to succeed against long odds: passion, vision, strategic thinking, tenacity, and just plain guts. Their story is inspiring—just like the view of Mount Baker from the top of the ridge, dazzling me during my memorable hike through the forest.

When board members from the Whatcom Land Trust (WLT) in Bellingham began talking about preserving a large parcel of land containing 750 acres of ancient forest around Canyon Lake Creek in 1993, they knew it contained old-growth trees—they just didn't know *how* old. According to a report jointly commissioned by the land trust and the landowner, a regional timber company looking to sell a portion of its

LEFT: Canyon Lake lies at the heart of the 2,300-acre community forest.

holdings, some trees were almost a thousand years old—alive during the Middle Ages. The report concluded that the parcel, including mountain hemlock, Pacific silver fir, and Alaska yellow cedar, and sitting at an altitude of between 3,400 and 4,400 feet above sea level, comprised one of the oldest intact forests in the Pacific Northwest. Not only had it escaped logging, but the stand had also survived the huge forest fires that devastated the Cascades region every three to four hundred years.

WLT board member Rand Jack learned these facts while reviewing the report on a long plane ride from Seattle to Chile. "As I read on," he recalls now, "the smile on my face grew larger. This report provided the compelling evidence the Whatcom Land Trust would need to win public support and to raise cash— more cash than we had ever before dreamed of raising." Before it was finished, the unassuming little land trust would have to raise more than $4 million.

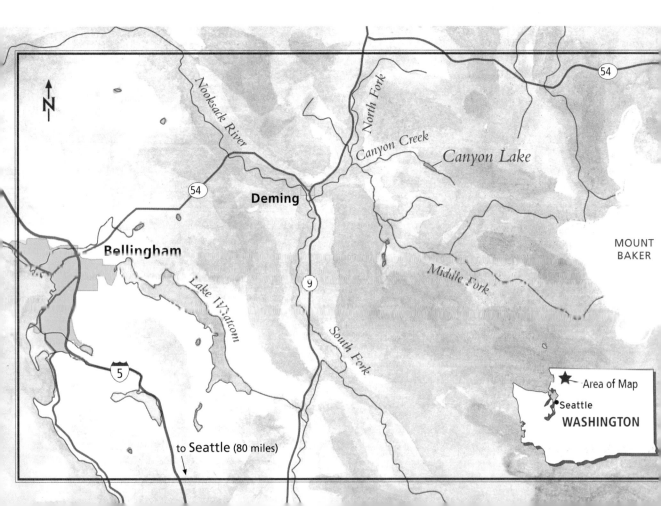

Starting Small

With a population of 170,000, Whatcom County is located about two hours north of Seattle. Bounded by 143 miles of Pacific Ocean coastline, three thousand miles of rivers and streams, and the spectacular Cascade Mountains, the county is also blessed with rich farmland. As growth spread northward from Seattle in the early 1980s, many people became concerned about the strain development would place on their rural community. In response, citizens formed the Whatcom Land Trust in 1984 to harness the energy and vision of those wishing to protect their treasured landscape and farmland.

Agriculturally oriented at first, the land trust soon protected three defining properties: the Herman Miller Farm, the spectacularly scenic Clark's Point along Puget Sound, and Chuckanut Ridge. Preserving these parcels greatly enhanced WLT's credibility as an effective and dedicated community nonprofit. Craig Lee, regional director of the Trust for Public Land's Northwest office in Seattle, was instrumental in helping to set up the land trust and oversee the Miller Farm conservation easement. As he told me, he soon lost a part of his heart to the land and people of Whatcom County.

The project to protect Canyon Lake Creek forest began to take shape in 1993, when WLT facilitated a large and complex land transaction known as the Great Land Exchange, involving both purchase and exchange of thousands of acres between the Trillium Corporation and various public owners. Some of the land became publicly owned and protected; other parcels shifted from the Department of Natural Resources to Trillium to consolidate timberland holdings. One of these parcels was 350 acres of Canyon Lake Creek old-growth forest. Understandably, WLT board member Rand Jack and conservation director Gordon Scott became anxious about losing the ancient forest to private ownership and, thus, potential logging. Gordon alerted Rand that the forest was, most likely, the largest block of privately owned old growth in Whatcom County. Just before

"We suspected these trees were old from informal ring counts we'd done on stumps in adjacent clear-cuts, but we couldn't really believe we were counting accurately."

the
Steward
Volume 12 Number 2   Newsletter of the Whatcom Land Trust, Bellingham, Washington   Summer 2002

Working Together to Protect the Lake Whatcom Watershed

Olsen Estate Adds to Watershed Protection

In a rare joint session, the Bellingham City Council and the Whatcom County Council met May 21 to accept from the Whatcom Land Trust an option to purchase the 369-acre Olsen Estate Property in the Lake Whatcom Watershed. The property is located across Lake Louise Road from Sudden Valley. The Land Trust obtained an option in March to purchase the forested property for $819,000. In this three-way partnership, the County and City own the property together, and the Land Trust holds a conservation easement protecting the property in perpetuity from development.

Land Trust president Wendy Walker hailed this transition as "the kind of cooperation that will be needed if we are to protect the watershed" and praised the City and County "for joining with the Land Trust in take this substantial and symbolic step."

After owning the property for sixty years and living there as somewhat of a recluse, Leila June Olsen died in 1991. She left no will and a long search turned up no heirs. Under such circumstances, the property passes to the State Department of Natural Resources. By law, heirs have seven years from the date of death to claim property. A few months before the redemption period expired, a professional bounty hunter located three distant relatives of Leila June Olsen. For a 15 percent commission, he told them of

"...the kind of cooperation that will be needed if we are to protect the watershed..."
— Wendy Walker, WLT President

their inheritance. A great grandfather had changed the spelling of Olsen from "e" to "o," which had thrown the original searchers off track. Ironically, one of the heirs is named Leila June Olson.

A court ordered the property returned to the estate, setting the stage for the Land Trust to secure an option to purchase. This project is exciting for a number of reasons:

• protects one of the largest privately owned blocks of land in the Lake Whatcom watershed

• strategically situated near the 350-acre Stimpson Family Nature Reserve (cover story in Winter-Spring 2001 *The Steward*).

• provides a great vehicle to demonstrate the power of working together with key partners to protect an invaluable resource.

The Land Trust thanks Theresa Scherurup, attorney for the Olsen Estate, for making this transaction work for the Land Trust and the people of Whatcom County.

— Rand Jack

ABOVE: WLT is very effective in conveying word of their accomplishments. After all, one can be doing great work, but if no one knows about it, how can they support you? **RIGHT:** This photo, taken by WLT board member Rand Jack, was key to engaging the public in the quest to save the ancient forest.

the land exchange was finalized, Rand—from the beginning, the primary proponent of the deal—spoke out at a stakeholder meeting of some forty people, opposing the transfer of old-growth forest in the Canyon Lake Creek Basin from public to private ownership.

To keep the transaction on track, Trillium pledged a good-faith effort to conserve the 350 acres of old-growth trees, agreeing to do nothing to diminish the forest without first consulting the land trust, and making a serious effort to find a conservation solution. However, with limited data available concerning the forest's integrity, it became obvious that objective opinions from forestry experts were essential. WLT and Trillium thus agreed to share the cost of hiring an independent consultant to study and report on the forest's composition. Their choice was renowned University of Washington forest ecologist Jim Agee, who routinely took core samples from the trunks of trees. The resulting discovery of the forest's advanced age was beyond anyone's greatest expectations. As Gordon Scott related to me, "We suspected these trees were old from informal ring counts we'd done on stumps in adjacent clear-cuts, but we couldn't really believe we were counting accurately. The numbers we got were *so* high; and it was very difficult to count such tight annual growth rings."

In 1997 Trillium Corporation announced its intention to sell most of its county timberland holdings, including Canyon Lake Creek, to Crown Pacific Timber Company, based in Portland, Oregon. Simultaneously, two other pivotal events occurred: Trillium granted an option to the Trust for Public Land to purchase 350 acres of old-growth trees acquired in the original 1993 exchange with the Washington Department of Natural Resources. And the Whatcom Land Trust created a partnership with the Trust for Public Land to pursue acquisition. Fortunately, Crown Pacific agreed right away to expand the option to include the full 750 acres of old growth in the upper Canyon Lake Basin. The price tag for the project would eventually reach $3,692,000.

RIGHT: (from left to right) Russ Pfeiffer-Hoyt, master trail-design artist; Gordon Scott, dedicated land conservationist and WLT staff member.

Thinking Big

Reports in hand, Rand and Gordon took their case to the land trust board for approval to move forward. "Although the decision was never in doubt," Rand recalls, "the board needed to raise our aspirations and meet a challenge far exceeding anything we had done in the past." Although some board members were skeptical of their ability to raise the daunting figure needed to buy the 750 acres, everyone shared in the determination to make every effort to do so. Long-time board member, Hilda Bajema, who exemplified the land trust's cautious and thoughtful approach to such an ambitious campaign with her trademark attention-to-detail style, gave her blessing after learning the elements involved. Gordon later remembered Hilda's broad smile as a signal that the Canyon Lake Creek project was about to become a bold new step for the land trust. Support

Complementary Promotional Tools and Tactics

To further engage people in the story of the forest and its significance to the community and to the environment, WLT board member Rod Burton developed an outreach folder filled with photographs and colorful inserts. The piece provided an excellent tool for presenting the project to the public, the media, potential funders, elected officials, and others.

In 1997 WLT board members Bob Keller and Rod Burton spearheaded publication of *Whatcom Places*, a beautiful book filled with essays and photographs reflecting the best of Whatcom County, with an introduction by renowned writer Ivan Doig. According to Rand Jack, "Bob Keller conceived it, organizing its creation in a wonderfully collaborative manner. Rod Burton represented the artistic force, doing the design and layout. Area artists donated all of the writing and photographs." The book was very effective in helping to focus and express the pride residents felt in the natural beauty of their county. In the process, it built support for the land trust and its projects, especially Canyon Lake Creek Community Forest.

Rand Jack's photograph of a young girl near one of the

forest's oldest and biggest trees also resonated as an evocative image. Video from news reports and press conferences added dimension to the visual and promotional collection. At a press conference to announce the Paul Allen Foundation gift, noted Western Washington University forest ecologist Jerry Franklin informed those attending about the characteristics and value of old-growth forests in general, and these trees in particular. His talk was captured on video and used to attract additional support. Jerry's generous participation as adviser and supporter educated everyone involved and added stature to the project.

But by far the most compelling tactic was taking people into the forest to witness it firsthand. Words and pictures helped, but standing next to the giant trees and appreciating their age and beauty brought invaluable results in terms of funding, publicity, and moral support.

came also from board member and retired history professor Bob Keller, a powerful voice for seeing the big picture from a long and rich perspective—in this case, the history of land and natural resource conservation in the Pacific Northwest. According to Gordon, "Bob's enthusiastic support for the project gave it an aura of inevitability and historical meaning."

Now WLT faced the challenge of raising public support and funding, in part by showing both the need and enthusiasm for this project to the elected officials who made the policy decisions involving millions of dollars. To capture the public's imagination, WLT found it had to expand its base of support south to Seattle. In November 1997, a timely and strategically placed article appeared in *The Seattle Times*. The article on the old-growth forest appeared in color and "above the fold," reflecting its regional importance and giving credibility to the effort. The story was published in part because of personal connections—Bill Dietrich, a former student of Rand Jack and Bob Keller, was science and environment editor at the paper—but more important, the subject excited the reporter and photographer assigned to cover it. The story drew significant and favorable attention, offering the real possibility of success for the first time to the land trust and the project.

The Trust for Public Land brought its considerable weight to the project as recipient of a sizable grant from the Paul Allen Foundation to acquire and preserve old-growth forest in the Pacific Northwest. While considering many other possibilities, TPL viewed the Canyon Lake Creek project as an ideal funding prospect. At that point, the forest included 750 acres of ancient trees, a forty-five-acre lake, fifty-million-year-old fossils, and more than a dozen streams.

Soon, a site walk was scheduled to introduce Paul Allen Foundation program officer Bill Pope to the forest. Believing the foundation to be one of their most important prospects, the partners waited anxiously for Bill's response; it was now or never. Standing together on an old logging landing looking out over the Canyon Lake Valley, they were astonished to hear Bill's emphatic opinion that the group was *thinking too small* in scope! He challenged them to expand their vision to include not only the 750 acres of old growth, but also the entire 2,300-acre upper Canyon Lake Creek Basin and the lake itself. For everyone present, it was a defining moment.

Later all agreed that having a "big thinker" like Bill was crucial to setting higher goals; and, as Rand Jack says, "It also helped that the person with a bigger vision also spoke for big money." After all, the will and the energy existed to accomplish something worthwhile for the whole community. Why not raise the bar, to aspire to even grander possibilities?

It is important to note the credibility and momentum that the resulting award of $1,846,000 from the Allen Foundation brought to both the land trust and the project. "Once we had support from the Allen Foundation," Rand says, "everyone had to take us seriously." Further, the contact would not have been made without the Trust for Public Land's help—at that time, through TPL project manager Chris Rogers.

Another person who contributed pivotal funding and energy to the project was Peter Stein of Lyme Timber Company, based in Lyme, New Hampshire. He played a critical intermediary role with two anonymous donors, who together contributed $1.3 million. Stein, a former longtime Trust for Public Land staff member, facilitates land conservation acquisition projects on a national scale for Lyme Timber. Over the years, he has developed extensive networks and contacts and is often called upon to help accomplish large and complex projects because of his many skills. Rand Jack asserts that, "Quite simply, without Peter, the deal would not have happened."

The land trust's next step was to approach Whatcom county executive Pete Kremen to ask for his support. Kremen, a former radio announcer, steps into his popular role as master of ceremonies at the land trust's annual auction fund-raiser, among his many other substantive contributions. His vote of confidence was especially helpful, because enlisting county elected officials as land conservation proponents could often be difficult. He proved to be among WLT's most enthusiastic advocates. He later told Rand Jack that his work to help acquire the community forest was probably the most important thing he did as county executive because of the value to all partners involved. His relationship with the land trust continues to this day.

Although by this point the land trust had raised $2,997,000 toward the purchase price (a figure reduced by $146,000 in a goodwill gesture by Crown Pacific), it still needed to raise $700,000. Time was running out; the option was due to expire in November of 1998. The members realized they needed county council support to appropriate funding from Whatcom County's Conservation Futures Fund—money raised through a special property tax levy and dedicated to open space and recreational land acquisition—but knew this wouldn't be easy. Many councilors were conservatively oriented and opposed to increasing government land ownership. Further, despite the recreation, education, and scientific components of this project, WLT feared that the wilderness preservation aspect might be featured too prominently for the council's taste. The council was, most likely, loath to reduce the tax base by having private land sold to a tax-exempt nonprofit, or to support anything with negative impact on the logging industry. To add to the difficulty, the Whatcom Land Trust had recently completed another transaction from the Conservation Futures Fund, requiring the largest expenditure ever. Chances for raising additional money seemed slim, but the need to bridge the funding gap loomed large.

The appeal of a community forest with ancient trees was difficult to ignore.

Facing a daunting task, the land trust focused on helping people envision a thousand-year-old community forest in order to build support and funding to acquire the land. It emphasized the important balance struck on the same parcel of land: respecting the forest by protecting a sacred place as a no-cut zone, while actively managing for timber production on adjacent land owned by Crown Pacific.

In addition to using Pete Kremen's influence, the land trust approached council members using a particularly effective strategy—through trusted mutual friends. The trust's board reviewed each council member's list of contributors, identifying those whom they knew best. They then paired board members with contributors, asking the donors to personally contact that councilor to enlist their support. Persuasive pitches thus came from enthusiastic campaign supporters, rather than from the land trust. A few weeks later, the council voted unanimously to support the project with $700,000. Success was at hand.

In Rand Jack's view, numerous factors contributed to the positive council vote. The land trust's credibility in the community was pivotal. It had raised almost $3 million from the private sector. The appeal of a community forest with ancient trees was difficult to ignore. A broad spectrum of community leaders supported the project. Council members visited the forest to experience it first-hand. A county fund, dedicated by law, was available to purchase conservation land. And Roger DeSpain, the hugely popular and respected parks director, did everything he could to support the project.

Clearly, personal connections built positive public and political support here. Also, the land trust presented a financing package that leveraged county funds with more than $3 million of other funding—a true bargain. Further, the non-confrontational land trust was politically safe to support. The resulting relationship of public and private entities was positive and synergistic for all involved.

During the process, Rand Jack approached Western Washington University, inviting them to join as partner and co-owner of the forest. He contacted Al Froderberg, WWU vice president and provost, asking him for a vote of approval by the trustees. Excited by the project, Froderberg took on the request himself, as the university president was out of town, resorting to an unusual vote-by-phone proxy. The trustees agreed, and WWU became a valued education-based partner, bringing added credibility and support.

To engage the public, the partners spent a good deal of time talking with groups and individuals, persuading them of the importance of the project through both words and images. "The idea of a thousand-year-old community forest became a powerful selling point," claims Rand Jack. "In addition to the environmental community, we gained support from the chamber of commerce, realtors, local loggers, the Bellingham City Council, building contractors, an investment firm, a grocery store chain, the local ARCO refinery, and the school board in the district in which the forest is located. This broad coalition made it difficult for the council to say no.

"Building community through owning and caring for a rare, ancient forest was an idea that reached out and drew people in," Jack continues. "The community forest concept combined the compelling themes of conserving an old-growth forest and building community. It harkened back to the notion of a village commons, a geographical place that helped unify the community and give it a sense of pride and shared meaning. Public ownership could help educate local people in the meaning and practice of stewardship. The community forest idea gave us a language with which to think about our project and communicate its richness to those from whom we would seek help."

Against the Odds

Without the collaboration of several key players, the results might well have been vastly different. Individually and collectively, these people were positive, thoughtful, collaborative, creative, politically savvy, and inclined to take risks. Four, in particular, exemplify these qualities.

Integral to the whole process was Rand Jack. An attorney, professor, wood sculptor, ardent conservationist, and longtime land trust board member, Rand has passion and energy that are tireless and infectious. During the campaign, he pressed on when the odds seemed insurmountable, buoyed by his firm conviction in the value of preserving this forest on so many levels. Over the years he

"Building community through owning and caring for a rare, ancient forest was an idea that reached out and drew people in. The community forest concept combined the compelling themes of conserving an old-growth forest and building community."

BELOW: Dana and Rand Jack took me on a memorable walk through the forest and up to the ridgetop. They also hosted me at their house, sight unseen. LEFT: One of Rand Jack's creations, in the works.

may well have contributed thousands of volunteer hours in support of various land trust projects. Rand and his wife, Dana, both professors at Western Washington University, spent countless hours in support of the community forest project. On a beautiful fall day, they guided me on a memorable hike through the forest, purposefully neglecting to alert me to the spectacular scenery at the top of the ridge so I could fully experience it as we came around the corner.

Roger DeSpain is the former director of the Whatcom County Parks and Recreation Department. DeSpain's problem-solving abilities—his "we'll take care of it" attitude, coupled with his enthusiasm—were key elements in ensuring the project's success and, in the process, creating one of the most significant county parks in the Pacific Northwest. Rand is clear in his praise for Roger: "Without him, this would not have happened. From the first phone call, he was bold, supportive, and excited. Faced with a proposal that would have screamed caution to most county parks directors, Roger immediately saw the vision. He went side by side with us to make it work." Roger also reassured county executive Pete Kremen and helped to win over the county council.

When we visited, Roger told me, "The Whatcom Land Trust has taken citizen involvement to a new level. They bring huge energy, ideas, and resources into the county parks system. They don't just make suggestions. They are right here with us, making things happen. This partnership may keep me on my toes, but being on your toes allows you to reach higher than you otherwise might have."

Russ Paul serves as land and timber manager for Crown Pacific. Russ was instrumental in facilitating the company's positive decision to sell the land as a community forest. As WLT's Gordon Scott says of Paul in his unique role, "He saw himself as part of the community, not just as a timber manager." His collaborative way of working served as an inspirational model for both sides of often

Leave It Alone

New perspectives generated by land conservation efforts can be surprising and ironic, as this ad for A.1 Builders in Bellingham demonstrates in the land trust newsletter: "Our company salutes Whatcom Land Trust for the richness they bring to this community by helping us all leave things alone."

"This partnership may keep me on my toes, but being on your toes allows you to reach higher than you otherwise might have."

opposing interest groups. When I spoke with him, he was complimentary of the partnership, noting how much it differed from others whose progress, all too often, he likened to "watching a glacier move." Russ noted the "gut-wrenching challenge" of negotiating with landowners to create access to the forest along a formerly private road. For this he had to conduct a title search back to the early 1900s, winnowing down from an original dozen to a handful of landowners who were rightly concerned about security, public access, and maintenance issues. He not only had to convince them all of the value of this project, but also to keep negotiations on track and within budget. His assurance that Crown Pacific would "carry the banner," curiously, reassured them. "Building relationships with those folks helped a lot, especially when you actually do what you say you will," he says. "They still call me with maintenance issues, even though the county has the responsibility."

As part of his job, Paul spends time at schools talking with students about forestry and the role of timber companies in maintaining healthy forests. He told me that many young people are not aware that timber companies actually plant trees after they log a forest. To him, this information gap remains the same as when he started in the industry thirty years ago. "Timber companies," he says, "still do not do a good enough job educating children, and therefore their parents, about the value of forestry to their lives and communities."

In a recent issue of the land trust's newsletter, *The Steward*, Paul was recognized as "a man of his word," referring to a promise he made before closing the sale of the 2,300-acre forest in the fall of 1998. Prior to the sale, Crown Pacific had removed a giant six-ton rock containing a fifty-million-year-old fossil, placing it at its headquarters in Hamilton, Washington. True to his vow to return the prehistoric fossil to its home, in June of 2002 Russ arranged for transport of the huge rock on a flatbed truck. It now sits about 150 yards up the trail from the parking lot, for visitors to enjoy as they hike by. As Rand Jack wrote in the

newsletter article, "This was another example of the respectful and dedicated manner in which people approached this project." And, by recognizing the honor involved in keeping his word, the land trust acknowledged the value and weight of personal integrity in successful community-oriented projects.

Russ Pfeiffer-Hoyt is a contractor specializing in building trails, using both engineering skills and artistry. According to many of the people with whom I spoke, Russ's creative way of designing the trail to honor the forest's sacredness, and in interpreting that sense both for the visitor and in balance with the leaders' original vision, made his contribution significant.

The trail he built winds up through the forest, passing by some particularly large and interesting trees he discovered along the way, giving visitors a glimpse at their sheer size and beauty. The trail culminates in the memorable view I saw from the top of the ridge—across to 10,777-foot Mount Baker and the nearby Twin Sisters. Yet as Russ explains it, his motives were multidimensional. "I started with the old-growth trail to showcase the forest. But I also wanted to leave a large area undisturbed for wildlife."

Pfeiffer-Hoyt's ultimate goal is to help people acquire a love of land from places in their own towns. "Until we stop moving and fouling our nests and realize that *this* is the land that forms us," he says, "we'll always be immigrants." (His own family originates from Norway.) He has been likened to a "master weaver in threading the trail through the forest tapestry, cutting no more than three or four trees as large as six inches in diameter."

The project partners envisioned trails as serving a variety of purposes—among them, reflection and renewal, recreation and education. By all accounts, Russ Pfeiffer-Hoyt's talent and sensitivity in giving form to the trail truly captured the essence of the original vision for the community forest.

As these four men came together to help make this project a reality, they built mutual respect and camaraderie, leading to other projects down the road. They were receptive to understanding philosophy or priority and often brought together differing points of view through good communication. At that time, conservationists did not often work with timber-company executives—a pattern that is, thankfully, changing. By demystifying often-held misperceptions and building trust, this group of men with widely diverging jobs found common ground, enabling them to move forward. Roger DeSpain summed it up well, telling me, "When I see Rand now I regularly ask, 'What's next?' "

Changing Styles

The success of the Canyon Lake Creek Community Forest project brought a multitude of positive changes to the community. It altered the way in which people there think about working together for a common purpose. Participation by the timber companies in this process showed they possessed "soul"—a term not often associated with corporate entities with singular economic focuses, often at odds with environmentalists and other activists. The project also bridged the gap of old-style environmentalism—typically the black-and-white, winner-takes-all, loser-gets-nothing outcome. Simply put, there is not enough money just to *buy* all the special places in our communities. Therefore, people must be able to work together so everyone wins, and, in the process, accommodate a variety of needs: philosophical, economic, environmental, and spiritual. Sharing a vision, with all the give-and-take that requires, ensures that when the project comes to fruition, everyone arrives at the same place together. As a result, Western Washington University and Whatcom County jointly own the forest, while the Whatcom Land Trust holds the conservation easement.

For Gordon Scott, participating in the project changed the way he viewed the world. "We needed to think big. This project was very big for our small corner of the planet, but it was doable. The biggest challenge was just *imagining* that we could do it. Once we actually decided, figuring out how was easy." He learned also that, "Good projects are easy to accomplish; they attract good partners and funding. But big projects also attract big funders." When I ask about his own key role, Scott is characteristically self-effacing. "It was to support Rand Jack, both tactically and strategically. But I also provided psychic support by threatening to lie down in front of the bulldozers if we couldn't find a way to protect the property." About Gordon, Rand says: "His work was absolutely indispensable to the creation of the Community Forest. He knows the land, understands the ecology, gains people's trust, and never lets ego get in the way of getting the job

WHATCOM LAND TRUST
FIVE-YEAR
CONSERVATION
AGENDA
1999 - 2004

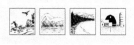

done. In a long, difficult project like this, filled with ups and downs and twists and turns, you could not ask for a more reliable, effective partner."

For seasoned negotiator Craig Lee, who oversaw the Trust for Public Land's important role from Seattle, "The outcome was pivotal, setting a precedent for creating a diversity of guardians and stewards for this miraculous place—one for which the land conservation movement lacks enough good examples. For me personally, the project represented a turning point. From now on I will try to find only the toughest, most challenging, and truly impossible land conservation projects to undertake."

Nevertheless, despite all the concerted effort, some events seemed almost divinely ordained. During one memorable press visit, a large helicopter happened to swoop down from the ridge carrying a giant tree dangling at the end of a chain. The timing could not have been more chilling, or more persuasive, in conveying the sense of urgency in saving some of the ancient, majestic trees before they were all gone.

Today, thanks to the vision of a few and the work of many, the Canyon Lake Creek Community Forest exists. Rand Jack speaks of a "sense of incredible privilege" from working on this project. "The implications are enduring, going far beyond us and our daily rounds and giving meaning to our lives." When walking through this special, sacred place, you can feel what he is talking about as you sense the passion, daring, and tenacity of a group of people with diverse but ultimately common interests, who came together to ensure its preservation for everyone, forever.

"Ten years ago I wouldn't have even talked to those people. But now we look for solutions

instead of ways to fight each other."

—Stoney Burk, attorney and committee member

4

The Rocky Mountain Front Advisory Committee

Choteau, Montana—*Former adversaries and longtime landowners find common voices and constructive solutions that help to maintain the deeply held way of life for ranchers in the West.*

This is a story about channeling passion for the land away from confrontational, head-butting warfare, and into productive collaboration. For decades conservationists in Montana had been regarded with skepticism and even outright hostility by large landowners. Then, in an inspired move, the local chapter of an international land conservation organization formed a local citizens advisory committee that allowed both sides, for the first time, to come together, to talk, to listen—and to take action to preserve the land they all loved.

Part of my soul has lived in Montana since I first spent time there in the 1970s, drawn by the larger-than-life landscape and the dramatic play of light across it. After talking with some members of the Rocky Mountain Front Advisory Committee of The Nature Conservancy, I realized how powerfully the people who live there embody the notion of "fierce love" of land. Though the East Coast—where I'm from—is historically "older," the common struggle of successive generations along the Front engenders a deeply rooted sense of pride and resourcefulness.

LEFT: "Fifteen grizzlies are probably watching us right now," says third-generation rancher and committee member, Karl Rappold.

Roughly one hundred miles long, the Rocky Mountain Front forms the eastern slope of the Rocky Mountains where they meet the Great Plains. In Montana, known as Big Sky Country, the wild lands along the Front are still largely unfragmented by human development—a feature uncommon in the lower forty-eight states. Except for bison, every creature that has roamed those plains

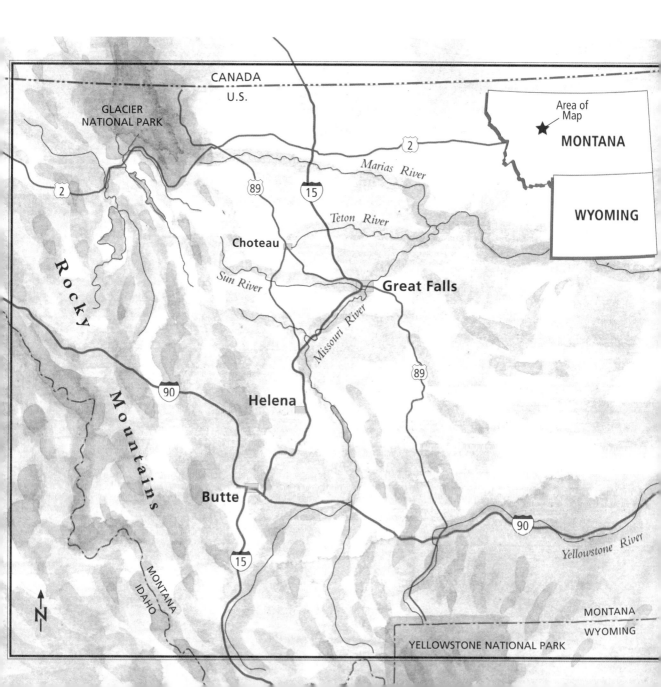

since Lewis and Clark's time in the early 1800s is present today (though admittedly in much smaller numbers): elk, antelope, mule deer, grizzlies, black bear, moose, wolves, and others. The Blackfeet people call this area "the backbone of the world."

The territory contains large ranches, many of them handed down over generations. Among the most pressing issues of this landscape for conservationists are the lack of fire in the ecosystem because of a policy of suppression, the protection of the unique native grasslands, special wetlands features, and grizzly bear habitat. But most pressing of all issues is habitat fragmentation due to rural subdivision. In the past two decades a wave of change has swept across the Intermountain West, centering on water, mineral, and grazing rights, and rampant development. Many of these long-held ranches changed ownership, often because high prices for open land were just too compelling to resist. Neighboring ranchers felt economically powerless to slow the pace of subdivisions. In response, several collaborative initiatives have surfaced, born of the desire to keep family ranches, livelihoods, wild lands, and a unique way of life intact. The Malpai Borderlands Project in New Mexico, the Devil's Kitchen group in Montana, the San Pedro River Partnerships in Arizona and Mexico, and the Yampa Valley Partners in Colorado are a few good examples (see Resources).

People in the rural West are famously independent. And they don't like outsiders telling them what to do. Therefore, the unusual convening of the Rocky Mountain Front Advisory Committee based in Choteau, Montana—a town of

1,800 people—illustrates well how much people who are traditionally on opposing sides of an issue can achieve by working together.

"Environmental Coup"

In 1978, the Montana chapter of The Nature Conservancy, an international conservation organization with offices in all fifty states and thirty countries worldwide, acquired the 13,000-acre Pine Butte Swamp Preserve and Guest Ranch. The purchase was viewed with skepticism by local residents, who saw it as an East Coast environmental coup, with the potential for more people coming in from afar to tell them how to live on and use their land. Here was a large and previously little known organization buying a sizable parcel from a longtime owner and altering its management by shutting down traditional ranching uses. Immediately, two things were in short supply: credible information and trust. Unfortunately, the initial preserve managers did little to help the situation. Keeping largely to themselves, they concentrated on the Conservancy's science-oriented mission. By the time co-managers Dave Carr and Mary Sexton arrived in 1989, they had many fences to mend. Nevertheless, they soon realized the value of becoming part of the community, and of being inclusive. Reactions and relationships began to change, but not without a lot of time and effort. This is the story of some of the key community people involved, and how they managed to get along.

By the time he became the Rocky Mountain Front Project Director, Dave Carr already was widely respected as a collaborative leader. More than one Advisory Committee member shared with me the belief that Carr's main interest lay in helping to benefit the ranching economy and to preserve its traditions and

A Landscape Influenced by Geology

The Rocky Mountain Front is comprised almost entirely of marine sediments from the ancient Cretaceous Sea, deposited during the latter part of the Mesozoic Era, between 65 and 135 million years ago. As this sea receded and the continents shifted along tectonic boundaries, mountain building resulted. With climate variation over the past several million years, continental ice sheets expanded from the poles. At the height of this glaciation, the North American continental ice sheet expanded south to just north of Choteau. Upon receding, it left large ice chunks in a gouged landscape that, when fully melted, left abundant small ponds or "prairie potholes." Today, fed by snowmelt, precipitation, and/or springs, these ephemeral and dynamic features wax and wane with the seasons and climatic conditions.

culture, and that his initial presence made the difference in encouraging them to participate.

Carr has lived in Montana for thirty years. Upon graduating from college in New Hampshire with a degree in forestry, he came to the Bitterroot Valley in southwestern Montana where he landed a job with the U.S. Forest Service working on fire and trail crews. Later, at the University of Montana, he received a degree in geology and, in the process, discovered landscapes—his life's dominant theme.

When he moved to the Bitterroot Valley in the early 1970s it was rural. "Now," he says, pointing out an irony, "it has been developed, partly because it is so beautiful there." As in other places, residents were concerned about planning and zoning to preserve their ranchland, but that concern unfortunately did not translate into action. With the influx of new residents from California, Washington, and Oregon, and the building of subdivisions, ranches disappeared in droves—prices there were just too good. To Carr, the Bitterroot and other valleys in western Montana are prime examples of unchecked development in a rural landscape. There, ranchers have learned the hard way about the need to protect the area from subdivisions if they want to keep their ranches intact.

Dave first came to the Rocky Mountain Front in 1976 with his then wife, Mary Sexton, a Choteau native. In 1989 they became co-managers of the Conservancy's Pine Butte Swamp Preserve. Mary has a long local family history—at the Choteau library hangs a distinctive photograph of her white-haired grandfather feeding turkeys. Mary left the Front for twenty years, living for a

BELOW: An earlier version of the committee; most members remain involved.

time in California but returning to conduct environmental education and outreach at Pine Butte.

"About ten years ago," Mary says, "we tried to get something like the Rocky Mountain Front Advisory Committee (called the Frontlanders) started, but people weren't ready for it." In fact, she says, people got all riled up, especially around the perceived threats to their private property rights. For this and other reasons, Mary and Dave realized they needed to handpick participants. And to be truly grassroots, they needed to include landowners. But because at that time most landowners lacked both a common purpose and a sense of urgency, the idea didn't get far.

Within a few years, however, a sense of urgency developed. Open land began disappearing at an alarming rate, as people moved away from more urban areas on both coasts. In Montana, other successful collaborative efforts, such as the Blackfoot Challenge and the Devil's Kitchen group, had come together to focus on subdivision issues and elk management, respectively. These projects set the stage for the Advisory Committee to take hold where the Frontlanders idea had fallen short.

While the seeds of collaboration planted ten years before seemed about to come to fruition, Mary realized the task would not be easy. The cattle market—the lynchpin of the economy—continued to be depressed. Mary knew that only practical solutions could be of real value to the ranchers. And she worried that, once again, attempts to collaborate with ranchers would be sabotaged: that "rabble-rousers would neither change, nor let change happen."

Shifting Focus

In 1997, a strategic change occurred at the Conservancy. At the time, Carr says, the staff began to realize they were acting largely in opportunistic fashion by responding to circumstances haphazardly and without addressing threats to the landscape strategically and holistically. In response, the Conservancy shifted from a preserve-sized scale to a broader, more landscape-scale focus. According to Carr, in addition to loss of habitat from subdivision, one of the most significant threats was landscape damage by new landowners lacking the knowledge of how to manage large ranches properly, in a biologically desirable way. Therefore, the focus was narrowed to five or six distinctive Montana landscapes—including the Front—and Dave Carr became the Rocky Mountain Front Project Director.

The impetus for the creation of the Rocky Mountain Front Advisory Committee came largely from Montana chapter director and collaborative land conservation pioneer, Jamie Williams. Williams was instrumental in the success of the Yampa

Valley Partners (see Resources), an innovative project undertaken in the late 1990s seeking practical ways of maintaining ranching livelihoods in Colorado. He knew firsthand the advantages of collective planning and action. Before beginning his own collaborative efforts, Dave Carr interviewed Williams, as well as John Cook from the Malpai Borderlands Project, to learn from their experiences.

In 1998, building on both successful and unsuccessful examples of collaborative land conservation, Carr formed an exploratory group to try the Frontlanders approach again. Once again, the ranchers reacted with skepticism and a strident defense of private property rights. Undeterred, Carr enlisted help from several ranching families he knew from his days as manager of the Pine Butte Swamp Preserve or from purchasing conservation easements on their ranches. "As a former land manager," he says, "I got to know these folks over the fence. This helped a great deal in building other relationships." Another factor that helped make collaboration possible, Carr says, was the Conservancy's recognition that the committee should be concerned with human as well as natural communities—an acknowledgment of human beings as part of the natural world.

To determine the appropriate landscape boundaries for committee jurisdiction, Carr and Missoula botanist Peter Lesica undertook a rapid ecological assessment. The two drove up and down the Front to get a better sense of its defining elements. The survey results suggested that the territory be bordered by the Missouri River on the south and by the Highwood River on the north, just below Calgary in Canada. It covered four counties in Montana—Lewis and Clark, Teton, Pondera, and Glacier—as well as the Blackfeet Indian Reservation and a number of municipal districts in Alberta, Canada.

The criteria for selecting the initial advisory group members were simple: each member had to have his or her own vision and be willing to work constructively, though everyone might not agree.

The process started with six people: Dusty Crary, Anne Dellwo, Wayne Gollehon, Stoney Burk (the lone attorney), Lisa Bay, and Karl Rappold. To give the

The criteria for selecting the initial advisory group members were simple: each member had to have his or her own vision and be willing to work constructively, though everyone might not agree.

group a better context in which to get started, Carr procured a grant enabling several group members to visit the Malpai Borderlands Project in New Mexico, along the borders of Mexico and Arizona. Formed by the Malpai Borderlands Group in 1993, this community-based ecosystem initiative sought to address threats to ranching by educating, searching for common ground, and collaborating with local, state, and federal agencies, universities, and environmental organizations (see Resources). To inform the increasing number of visitors wishing to learn more, Ranching Today, a landowner/ranch program, was created. The Malpai Group addressed issues including shrinking open space in the Southwest, growing opposition to ranching, understanding ranching values and way of life, the increase in subdivision developments, improving grazing lands, coordinating fire control management, and dealing with the effects of recent droughts.

Committee members drove around the project area together in a van for three intensive days, learning about the elements of collaboration and talking about putting the knowledge to use in their own vision for the Front. For Carr, the trip became the single most important catalyst (although the full measure of it was unanticipated, Carr says) for the Rocky Mountain Front Advisory Committee. Together, participants came away from their visit with the Malpai Group with enthusiasm for creating their own version of an effective working committee. By 1999 they were ready to get started.

Initially, the Advisory Committee chose merely to advise The Nature Conservancy, but reserved the right to become a separate entity in the future. It decided to create a list of practical tools, and for the past five years it has worked on the following issues:

- *Conservation easements* placed through the sale of development rights, which afforded capital to ranchers for making needed improvements to buildings and stock. (The first successful easement offered a model for others to follow.)
- *Block management for hunting*, which enabled landowners to receive income from the state proportionate to the number of people they allowed to hunt on their land. As an inducement to protect public hunting opportunities on private lands, the Montana Department of Fish, Wildlife & Parks can pay a landowner for entering in the Block Management Program based upon the number of hunters/days they allow in a season. The department will also help (or completely) manage the hunting for a landowner.
- *Conservation real estate*, which has brought in conservation-minded people as real estate buyers to keep land open in large parcels, and in use as working ranches.
- A proposed *"conservation beef" program*, which involves raising and marketing open-range cattle as an alternative to traditional feedlot beef, and might create a profitable niche.
- *Grassbanking*, a program through which acquiring or leasing adjoining ranches for grassland rotation allows pastures to rest between grazing periods and seasons.
- *Weed eradication*, which consists of concerted efforts to remove invasive species that diminish the quality of grasslands.

During those first few years, the group tested a variety of programs. When one rancher's land burned during a wildfire, the group contacted several other landowners who had not used their grassland for various reasons, exchanging grazing rights for the land-management benefits of grazing and such services as new fencing. All sides agreed that the mutually beneficial solution of grassbanking created good land stewards; thus, the program began to be successfully implemented along the Front. Still, not all the ideas worked out well. Dave Carr reports that the conservation beef program has languished, partly because ranchers have not been able to acquire enough cattle with the proper credentials to make the numbers work.

Working Together

Advisory Committee members brought diverse histories and perspectives to the table. Some were Montana natives; others were from either side of the country. What they shared was the willingness to try to work together, tough as the

The Rocky Mountain Front Advisory Committee of The Nature Conservancy

(This is a good example of creating a mission statement, and parameters for committee structure, work, and conduct.)

The purpose of establishing a Rocky Mountain Front local advisory committee for The Nature Conservancy is to ensure that our work on the Front is responsive to the needs, concerns, and visions of the communities along the Front. The committee will work with the Conservancy to establish a program that conserves the Rocky Mountain Front and its habitat in a way that is compatible with the economic and cultural needs of the people and communities who depend on ranching as a livelihood along the Front.

Roles and Responsibilities

Committee members will be asked to advise the Conservancy on all of its activities on the Rocky Mountain Front, including the following:

1] **Community Outreach:** Advise the Conservancy on a strategy for making its work community-based, and for reaching out to specific interests on the Front; help involve other people in the project when appropriate for accomplishing specific tasks.

2] **Economic Development:** Explore economic opportunities that will benefit local ranchers and the communities in which they live, and that are compatible with the conservation of the Front's biological diversity.

3] **Acquisitions, Easements, and Management Agreements:** Advise the Conservancy on the desirability of conducting specific acquisitions, easements, and/or management agreements; advise on how best to structure these deals so that they are compatible with the local community.

4] **Stewardship Projects:** Help the Conservancy continue to develop a stewardship program that will achieve native grassland and riparian conservation that is compatible with ranching.

5] **Demonstration Projects:** Help the Conservancy establish projects that will generate new information on how specific economic uses and conservation of biological diversity can be best achieved together. Help the Conservancy devise methods for dispersing this information to the community.

6] **Management of Conservancy land:** Advise the Conservancy on managing individual parcels of Conservancy land to promote the health of specific plant and wildlife communities, and to meet other historic and community goals on those properties where appropriate.

7] **Fund-raising:** Advise the Conservancy on how to build support for specific projects.

In advising the Conservancy, the committee should be aware of the Conservancy's basic mission and philosophical principles that guide all of its efforts in the State of Montana.

Basics for Serving on the Committee

1] Interest in The Nature Conservancy's work on the Rocky Mountain Front, conserving the health of the ecosystem and biological diversity.

2] Interest in balancing the ecological needs of the Rocky Mountain Front with the economic and cultural needs of the Front's residents.

3] Willingness to attend quarterly meetings and advise The Nature Conservancy on an informal basis outside of meetings.

4] Common courtesy for other people's perspectives and a desire to work toward solutions.

going might get. In speaking with a few of them, I began to realize and respect the enormous courage and dedication they brought to bear. A sampling of committee members follows.

Stoney Burk is an attorney, artist, photographer, and former Vietnam fighter pilot. His wife runs the Outpost Deli in Choteau, where locals congregate every day to discuss just about anything of note. His clients are mostly ranchers, but he also does real estate work. Clients first asked for his help with conservation easements ten years ago. Sometimes he works with ranchers approached to sell land or easements by a federal agency such as the U.S. Fish & Wildlife Service. "In the early days," Burk recalls, "easements were pushed by government agencies. They could be pretty heavy-handed in their approaches." In response, in the early 1990s a sagebrush rebellion took place. "Since then," he says, "people in those agencies have learned about the mutually beneficial relationship between the landowner and the easement holder." With this added knowledge and understanding—plus the ability to negotiate—ranchers, government employees, and conservation organizations working together have made easements more practical and helpful. In fact, he notes, conservation easements often help family ranches pay off debt and make needed improvements to their land, buildings, and stock.

He is concerned that economic hardship has caused a steady loss of what he calls "our rural heritage"—truly an important part of our national heritage. His interest, therefore, lies in finding ways to preserve large, scenic, contiguous tracts of land to preserve both permanent and migratory life, as he knows it, along the Front.

Building trust among all sides has been slow until recent years, according to Burk. "Adding fuel to the fire," he says, was the fact that "initially conservation organizations bought productive ranchland and sold it to government entities. The ensuing public pressure between locals, conservation organizations, and government made people realize the tremendous hostility focused on the

"My great-grandfather spent his first two winters here living under his wagon."

buy-up of land. To locals, conservation appeared to be a front for the government." As for The Nature Conservancy, Burk says, "They needed to change their image, find common ground with ranchers, and to show real intention, so the organization began purchasing conservation easements instead of acquiring property outright." These days, the Conservancy buys land to sell only to individuals interested in keeping it as working ranchland, while reserving conservation easement rights and preserving habitat. Now a neighboring rancher often can affordably buy the land at a rate minus its full development value—a win-win scenario. "When the Conservancy and others began to listen more to local opinions by creating our committee, they provided the mechanisms to help foster success," he concludes.

Serving on the committee with Burk is Karl Rappold, a third-generation rancher who looks as if he would fit right into the seven movies he's worked on—all filmed in the area. On several he's played a cowboy, doing what he does best. He lives with his wife, Teri, on their 7,000-acre ranch. They lease an additional six thousand acres. Their grown children live in Montana, Utah, and Oregon. Rappold's great-grandfather came to Montana from Germany as a "grubstaker" in the 1880s. Upon arriving he received the standard three hundred acres of land with which to make a go of it. As Rappold says, "My great-grandfather spent his first two winters here living under his wagon." (Please keep in mind that winter temperatures on the Front regularly fall below minus-thirty to minus-forty degrees Fahrenheit, with the winds howling. What's more, he had two Norwegian mail-order brides. The first one didn't last. One hardly wonders why!)

When Dave Carr formed his exploratory group, he asked Karl Rappold to join, having met him through a bear-biologist colleague. On the strength of the others involved, the rancher agreed. Nevertheless, he insists, as does Stoney Burk, "It was very controversial for me to take that stand by participating." But through the shared process, he explains, "I began to view the people on the committee as individuals, even if I didn't always agree with them." Rappold was one of the original members visiting the Malpai Borderlands Project. There, he was struck by the friendliness and helpfulness of the people he met; and how, by being collaborative and successful, they had bucked the odds. As a group of fairly isolated ranchers, they had learned to get along and work well with government agencies, traditionally not an easy task in either New Mexico or Montana.

In a series of transactions between 1999 and 2003, and with the help of attorney Stoney Burk, Rappold sold conservation easements and traded land to The Nature Conservancy and the U.S. Fish & Wildlife Service. "This complex undertaking achieved great conservation while allowing Karl to expand his ranch in an area where typical ranchers can no longer afford to buy land," Dave Carr observes.

"I live what I love"

Rappold currently sells his beef on the Internet. Here on this big, beautiful, and seemingly remote ranch, a viable market for its cattle exists in cyberspace. According to his wife, Teri, who handles the marketing, "This method provides a much larger selection of buyers. Instead of hauling the cattle to a local livestock market, the cattle are videotaped on the ranch. The buyers can bid on them from home instead of coming out to Montana. This way hundreds of buyers from all over the country can have a chance to bid on the cattle, rather than just a few local ones. This way we are getting top market price."

These days the most efficient way to see the Rappold land is by truck. Across the valley about forty minutes away from the ranch buildings and through a number of gates sits the newest parcel, acquired with the help of the Conservancy. It is forested land beside a meadow with a clear, cold creek running through it, butting up against the mountains and offering a stunning vista. "Right now about fifteen grizzlies probably are looking down on us," Rappold tells me as we arrive. "A week ago a couple of them came out right near where I was showing the place to a couple from Italy. They were so excited to see them." He mentions that Dave Carr often brings potential donors to this spot—this is also Carr's favorite place.

Perhaps partly because of this new addition to his ranch, Karl Rappold no longer hunts. Now he can see big animals and appreciate them differently. After all, he says, "We are the trespassers on the Rocky Mountain Front. Bear, elk, and wolves were here long before my great-grandfather came." Last fall a National Public Radio reporter interviewed him against this spectacular backdrop to get his views on the oil and gas drilling proposals threatening both the Front and his own land. Shuddering at the thought, he tells me, "They'd have to put in a road big enough to get sixty tractor-trailer loads of equipment up there. It would destroy this place." When I ask if this might be where he'd want to be buried, Karl looks over and nods at me, pointing to a grassy knoll with a panoramic view of the entire valley. Sometimes when the wind is really blasting—upwards of 145 mph—he says he has to hold on to his truck just to stay upright. That wind can

sometimes even lift his heavy pickup off the ground. Here, Karl most strongly feels the power of his family's heritage. He works the ranch by himself, with help from his brother—and the work is endless. But he loves the land, the bears, and his horses. "I live what I love," he says. "And I don't 'work' for a living."

Advisory committee member Lisa Bay lives on the 4,000-acre Bay Ranch in Wolf Creek, about sixty miles south of Choteau, with her husband, Mike. They share the ownership of the ranch with Mike's mother. Bay's mother's family homesteaded in western Montana, west of Missoula, and she had seven siblings. Lisa, herself, grew up near San Francisco. "Every summer I spent a month with my favorite aunt in Superior, Montana, and it was the best part of growing up," she tells me. "So when I graduated from college [with a degree in environmental planning] and got offered a job as a county planner in California, I suddenly decided to throw it all in. I loaded up my El Camino and drove to Helena. A month later I brought my horse up. That was twenty-six years ago."

Bay joined the Advisory Committee as a rancher in 1999. She soon became invaluable, prompting The Nature Conservancy to hire her as staff in 2001. Although she works in that capacity for the Montana chapter, she voluntarily serves unpaid for her time spent on Advisory Committee work. When asked to list some of the positive results occurring since the committee's formation, she notes that its presence has helped to secure funding from public sources to accomplish needed conservation, including a new grassland reserve program. Another important benefit is the creation of a strong conservation culture on the Front, including support for initiatives supporting both ranching *and* conservation. The committee's presence has helped to build a bridge between locals and conservation organizations, and to encourage members to go out into the community to talk with others about their views. Further, it has established an effective vehicle for identifying economic tools or initiatives to help ranchers with productivity and income.

Since joining the committee, Bay has noticed her own evolution. She now makes sure she really "checks in" at meetings, being mindful of all points of view and making certain that everyone is acknowledged. She'll call on others to help her make personal connections, instead of just heading out herself, citing the added value of a team effort. When I ask about possible improvements to the process, she responds, "I think it would be good to sit down with everyone to see if they are satisfied with their progress. If not, what would they suggest? I also think that the committee should be staffed, to keep it running, to do follow-up work and keep the process organized."

In Bay's opinion the committee has created a new peer group. "These deeply committed people have gained the chance to have their feelings supported." As she says, "They now know that others, too, will lie down and die for conservation values for their land." She is impressed by "how many committee members have become articulate spokespeople for what they believe." For example, Karl Rappold now participates in Bureau of Land Management tours to share his conviction that oil and gas drilling are not appropriate on the Front. "This is a group of amazingly fine individuals," Lisa says. "They are genuinely nice—the kind of people I want to spend time with, even though I only know them in this context."

Committee member Lyle Hodgskiss is a thoughtful, pragmatic, and enthusiastic man, a native son of Choteau. He's both a rancher and a banker, whose ancestors came from England in the late 1880s, and whose family has homesteaded on their ranch since 1904. Originally 160 acres in size, the current ranch comprises 6,200 acres, with an additional 1,200 acres leased from the state. Lyle's dad made him "go away" to other parts of Montana to get an education for at least four years before deciding whether or not to continue ranching. The younger Hodgskiss soon extended that hiatus to eighteen years, building a career in banking. He is grateful for the time to gain added perspective. "Ranches are such huge assets," he tells me. "The people who will be operating them need to be able to think about the commitments they will be making." Since returning to Choteau, he has successfully maintained his banking career along with his ranch.

". . . the recreational or investment-minded buyer simply has no—or very few—emotional ties to the land or the community, or to the ranching culture along the Front."

Hodgskiss was an early Advisory Committee member, joining just before the reconnaissance trip to the Malpai Borderlands Project. Somewhat skeptical at first, he remembers wondering if the excursion would prove worthwhile. He was game to find out, though, and was glad he did, because the trip changed his mind. Of the New Mexico visit, he recalls, "The project gave us a vision of what a group of people with passion and energy can do." Nevertheless, he insists, passion and energy aren't enough without structure. Though he cautions, "They cannot be motivated solely by financial means either." He was particularly interested to learn about the grassbanking concept. "During hard times," he says, "ranchers tend to use their land very hard by necessity. Grassbanking allows the land to rest."

In Hodgskiss's opinion, most third-generation ranchers would be reluctant to sell. But once people get past the horror of giving up their family legacy and actually sell their land, he is concerned that newer owners will have an easier time selling to the highest bidder. "The reason," he claims, "is that the recreational or investment-minded buyer simply has no—or very few—emotional ties to the land or the community, or to the ranching culture along the Front." He speaks of a well-known, high-end appraiser in the state who contends that, for most buyers, the novelty of owning a ranch in Montana lasts approximately five years. After that time, apparently, the romance wears off to the point where people often lose interest and realize that the ranch is a very poor cash-flow investment. Subsequently, they sell the property. "If this holds true along the Front," he tells me, "we may begin to see some of the ranches purchased in the last five to seven years go back on the market. In order for owners to realize a respectable return on their investment, they would likely need to sell to developers for subdivisions, or parcel out the property themselves." Hodgskiss feels that the committee must come to grips with this reality.

He thinks the committee will most likely require some "small, distinct wins" to keep the momentum going. Still, he is amazed, as are most people, by the consistently high attendance record since the committee's inception. In praising the Conservancy he tells me, "They have been open-minded enough to perceive that ranchers aren't harming their land and that everyone shares the same goals."

Hodgskiss brings much of the necessary sensibility and structure to the table—or as he calls it, "a little reality." His practical knowledge—coupled with his business acumen, number-crunching ability, and orientation toward the economic value of proposed ideas—serves him well. Ranchers may not care much about conservation, but they do care about prices, he says, stressing the importance of finding ways to connect the two elements. He suggests that "ranchers need to be better versed in estate planning, since succession plays such an

important role in sustainability." And they can always do a better job of creating
a sense of community. But he is pleased to report that "when we have a meeting, everybody shows up. They really do care."

"You've got to get all the stars lined up"

Dusty Crary has a wealth of colorful stories up his sleeve. A former rodeo star
and champion bronc rider now in his forties, he has performed across the country. He lives on the ranch with his wife, Danelle, also a former rodeo performer,
and their three young children. Crary's grandfather—an Iowa dentist—acquired
the ranch in 1906, after reaching the end of the rail line in Choteau. There he
set up his dental practice. He later passed the ranch down to Dusty's father, who
spent his boyhood there, and returned after serving in the Korean War. Today

Crary owns the 2,000-acre ranch with his older sisters. He plays the primary role in day-to-day operations and leases additional land for his cattle to graze. He also guides hunting pack trips, lobbies the Montana legislature, and serves on nonprofit boards, in addition to raising a family. He is rarely still.

Crary met Dave Carr and Mary Sexton when they managed the Pine Butte Swamp Preserve. As he remembers it, "Before Dave and Mary came, Pine Butte was a preserve with a moat around it—off limits!" Asked about his own experience, Crary tells me, "No apparent threats to our way of life existed until about ten or fifteen years ago, when we started seeing a lot more houses back by Eureka Lake. We knew then we had to act." Suddenly encroached upon by people moving in next door on small tracts of land, the Crarys wanted to secure the integrity of their ranch before it was too late. As a result, in 1998 and 1999 the family worked with Carr and the Conservancy to place one of the first conservation easements in the area on their ranch. As a result, Crary became an original Advisory Committee member.

Crary has an insightful historic perspective. "In the fifties and sixties," he says, "agriculture had some really good years. Nobody meddled with the ranchers, and they became very independent. Finally they had achieved some prosperity. The resistance to environmentalists—and pointing fingers at them—is a relatively recent phenomenon."

Crary is adamant that "the younger generation get creative, open their minds and diversify enough to make this all work." In his words: "Compromise is the solution. Maybe you just don't get everything you want." With regard to the Advisory Committee's successful collaboration, he suggests the secret ingredient: "You've got to get all the stars lined up—right time, right people."

Some policies enacted in Washington, D.C., have big effects on life in Montana, Crary says. For example, the Endangered Species Act protecting large carnivores such as grizzlies has resulted in a lot more bears around the ranch. Dusty and Danelle must be careful with their young children, even at close distances from the house. But he has come to appreciate seeing grizzlies and knowing they are a part of life at the ranch. He claims he's gotten pretty enthusiastic about a grand regional plan called "Y to Y," establishing contiguous wildlife habitat corridors from Yellowstone to the Yukon.

As Crary's natural leadership skills emerged during his committee work, the Conservancy invited him to join its board. Proud to serve, he calls himself, "the first dirt-ball rancher trustee of the Montana Chapter." Recently he was elected vice chair. One senses that if only he had more time, he could be elected to just about anything. Ever optimistic, especially since spending time on the Advisory Committee, Dusty tells me, "The number of hard-line people is dwindling. People are more interested in being open and constructive these days. And every year you get a few more people to be more open-minded, accepting and tolerant of other people's opinions—even respectful. Even if that's all you've got when you go to the table, that's all you need."

The "good news" about the Front, Crary claims, is that it is "just a little too harsh and brittle—not desert—but with no big trout water. Winters are cold and windy but without a predictable snow pack to make it attractive as a ski resort location. So I get most excited about the prospect that this landscape will look relatively the same in the future. The culture will remain the same here. Good values, cultures, and land worth preserving. So far this is a success story. And after four years, we are still motivated and fired up."

Anne Dellwo is a fourth-generation rancher whose great-grandfather on her father's side started in ranching in 1890. Anne and her husband, Larry, have raised two sons, both of whom carry on the ranching tradition with growing families of their own. She is a slight woman, but her size belies years of hard but rewarding work spent keeping the ranch in her family. Her mother's family also came to the area in 1890—her parents met when they were eight. Today the ranch encompasses around twelve thousand acres, including several dwellings, a remote cabin, and many outbuildings.

Anne Dellwo is an original Advisory Committee member. She remembers when the Peebles family sold some land to The Nature Conservancy in 1985—the first locals to do so—in prime grizzly bear habitat along the Teton River. They received many negative phone calls about "selling out." Fortunately, things have changed, she says. By selling a conservation easement, the family was able to acquire her grandfather Knowlton's adjoining four thousand acres. At first the family had contemplated subdividing to raise the necessary capital. But Dave Carr convinced them to sell the development rights instead through a conservation easement, enabling them to afford the Knowlton land while protecting their own.

Dellwo is active as a district director for the Teton County Cattlewomen, a nonprofit organization that promotes cattle ranching as a way of life. She is a director of the Old Trail Museum in Choteau, which promotes tourism and dinosaurs, including the nearby Egg Mountain site, where a nest with duck-billed dinosaur eggs was found several decades ago. She says she is particularly interested in the Old North Trail, a travel route from Asia along the Siberian Strait to Mexico, used for ten thousand years by indigenous peoples. She belongs to an informal group that helped mark the trail with rocks as it passes through Teton County along the edge of the Front, to ensure that the route would not be lost to future generations.

Running the family ranch requires periodic extra labor, especially during the demanding calving season that begins each February and lasts three months. "During calving," she explains, "the whole family works together: my sons, their wives, our grandchildren, Larry and me." They are up every two hours all night long to stay abreast of all the cows giving birth. The harsh winter climate would otherwise quickly claim newborn calves. As the seasons change, the Dellwos move to different homesteads on the ranch. In the summer they live closer to the mountains. In the fall and early winter they return to the valley, guided mostly by seasonal rhythms and the demands of ranch life.

A Solid Foundation

Despite consistent participation by Advisory Committee members, the course hasn't always been easy. They have had to learn some important lessons along the way. In the spring of 2003, the Conservancy received negative publicity when *The Washington Post* disclosed certain policies employed by the national office concerning board and member practices favoring insider land purchases and resulting tax deductions. These procedures have since been substantially modified and clarified, but at the time chapters across the country braced for the fallout. Partly over this issue, the Rocky Mountain Front Advisory Committee lost two members, including an organic farmer originally from the East who, most agree, brought a great deal to the mix. By most accounts he is still missed. In general, though, most people concur that the committee's solid foundation, built over time on trust and mutual respect, helped it weather the storm. The relationships formed withstood the damaging reports from the opposite side of the country. In fact, this resiliency has proved to be the case for most state chapters—long-term connections transcended short-term difficulties, much like a marriage. Of the recent difficulties at the national level, Stoney Burk comments that, "While people are disappointed, they cannot afford to lose sight of the overall goal of saving their heritage and the last wild places."

In the years since Dave Carr and Mary Sexton served as preserve managers
at Pine Butte Swamp Preserve, general community participation has improved
dramatically. Some of this evolution is, no doubt, attributable to the example
offered by the Rocky Mountain Front Advisory Committee. Mary is now the
newly appointed director of the Montana Department of Natural Resources
and Conservation. Formerly she was a county commissioner for Montana's
Teton County, specializing in land use and comprehensive planning. In that
capacity she worked on growth management policy—a focus of timely significance, helping to guide development, transportation, and creation of conservation
lands and open space. Other positive changes have taken place too, especially in
how people accept both the Conservancy and project manager Dave Carr. As
Carr tells it, for twenty-five years he has been part of the community, raising
a daughter and earning his credentials. During that time, he notes, a genera-
tional shift has occurred. "People in the early days of the rural West were a
tough, independent bunch by necessity," he says. "The next generation has
traveled further afield. They realize they have to be able to work together now
to survive. They are more aware of the uniqueness of the Front. They have seen
unchecked development devour territory to the west—in the Bitterroot, and to
the south in Bozeman. And they realize they have to do something."

When Carr began to form the Rocky Mountain Front Advisory Committee,
he thought the results would prove formulaic, with certain expected outcomes;
yet many unintended but beneficial results have surfaced. He has learned about
the community members' depth of feeling for their landscape, how important
it is to their lives, and how they are willing to battle for it. He has seen personal
growth in the committee members, too. They are more open-minded now. The
conversation around land conservation has deepened. Members have become
activists, lobbying and sharing their beliefs more widely. Last year when Karl
Rappold traveled with fellow rancher Dusty Crary to the state capitol in Helena
to testify before the legislature on the value of conservation easements to ranchers, they did so with firsthand knowledge. The bill to abolish easements was
soundly defeated. Case closed. From this experience, Dave Carr has learned how
important one's integrity, and one's word, are in rural communities.

For Stoney Burk, "Serving on this committee has been a good way for people
like me—those with a healthy mistrust for government based on prior experience—to sit at a table together, to talk rationally about concerns and work out
solutions. It has offered a forum for more cordial and educational exchanges of
ideas. We've all learned. We better understand what challenges small ranchers

face. We better understand the constraints on government agencies and organizations. We are looking for solutions instead of ways to fight each other. We are looking more toward complementing each other."

Because the committee is run democratically, room exists to consider all opinions. Input from members helps Carr shape conservation actions—which, in turn, must be carried out in ways the members can live with. He is particularly pleased that, as a result, the ranchers are practicing ecologically sound methods appropriate for the landscape. And, by combining ranches, they are reassembling the landscape. Also of interest is the fact that grizzly bear recovery and wide-open landscapes are the issues attracting the most funding and activist support from people across the country.

This experience also has been transformational for Carr personally, by helping him to feel less isolated. He has gained wonderful friends. For example, prior to having Dusty Crary join the committee, Carr worked with him to place an easement on the Crary ranch. The two learned they share a love for the mountains, and Dave has since been on several Conservancy pack trips guided by Crary. Dave has also learned about patience, using early advice given to him by Montana director Jamie Williams about "going slow to go fast." Carr says his best tactic is to "lead from behind," letting committee members take their place out in front. He figures that this process is a good investment because with generations of knowledge comes a higher quality of land stewardship. And, he adds, "The educational aspect has been a two-way effort. I've probably learned more about conservation and love of the land from this group than I've ever passed on." The committee members have learned to listen well and consider other people's opinions. They have learned from each other's ideas and, in the process, have gained respect for one another and for the mission of The Nature Conservancy. They understand firsthand that local citizens can make a difference in preserving their land and, consequently, their way of life. And as a result of their participation, they have become invaluable advisors.

Before the committee was started, individuals felt they were each a voice in the wilderness. Joining together has taken them to a whole new level of advocacy as conservationists. Last fall, Karl Rappold spoke out eloquently on the gas and drilling issue for yet another *Washington Post* article. The piece, along with his photo, was carried in newspapers across the country. I noticed it with pride in my hometown newspaper in Maine. In the months afterward, he was quoted again several times. And just this fall, word came from Washington that the proposed drilling was to be suspended for at least three years to give more time to explore the potential buyout or trade-out scenarios for leases. According to Dave

Carr, this action was fueled, in part, by the hard work of, and strong sentiments expressed by, committee members Karl Rappold, Stoney Burk, Dusty Crary, and Roy Jacobs, "who got involved and put a community face to the voices of opposition that had not been there before." Even more recently, the U.S. Fish & Wildlife Service announced its intention of creating a large conservation easement program on the Front—an idea nurtured, discussed, and lobbied for by The Nature Conservancy and the Rocky Mountain Front Advisory Committee. Significant events and outcomes are beginning to occur here.

These are salt-of-the-earth people who live what they love, speak their minds, and hold their convictions passionately. They possess priceless senses of humor. They are resourceful, generous, and hardworking. They need to be to survive the harsh conditions imposed upon them by weather and geology. By working together, they've learned to listen, to accept people as individuals, and to change their points of view when necessary. Yes, much still needs to be done, but the groundwork is laid, the participants are in place. The big sky is the limit now.

"This community has what everyone is looking for all over the country."

—Sara Phelps, sales and marketing manager for the Eastern 4-H Environmental Education Center

5

VISION 2000: THE TYRRELL COUNTY ECONOMIC DEVELOPMENT INITIATIVE

Tyrrell County, North Carolina—*Citizens of diverse backgrounds help a southern, rural, coastal county to reclaim its heritage, guided and supported by the state chapter of a national conservation organization.*

This is a story of resourcefulness, featuring an innovative and multi-faceted rural revitalization project in Tyrrell County, in eastern North Carolina. Tired of being passed over for decades by tourists traveling to nearby beach resorts, citizens representing the public, private, and non-profit sectors met to envision new ways of working together, and to capture much-needed income for their county, using natural resources as the driving factor. For the people of this rural community, who often thought of themselves as backward in comparison to their urban counterparts, the experience was life-changing.

Tyrrell County lies in eastern North Carolina, on a peninsula between the Pamlico and Albemarle Sounds, on the way to the historic Outer Banks resort towns of Manteo, Kill Devil Hills, and Nags Head. During vacation season, thousands of people drive through the county every day. One might think this wayside location would attract curious visitors—but until recently, people rarely stopped.

With fewer than 4,500 residents, Tyrrell is North Carolina's most sparsely populated county. Out of one hundred counties in the state it is also the poorest—unemployment lingers around 20 percent. The population is 45 percent black and 55 percent white. Tyrrell County also has an emerging Hispanic population of one-time migrant farm workers who have taken up residence, and a growing Vietnamese population working in commercial fishing.

Located on the Atlantic Flyway, the county's peat wetlands and riverine swamp forests provide critical habitat for migrating birds and resident species such as the red wolf, bald eagle, American alligator, peregrine falcon, and the red-cockaded woodpecker. Notably, it sits at the center of seven national wildlife refuges: Alligator River, Cedar Island, Lake Mattamuskeet, Pocosin Lakes, Roanoke River, Pea Island, and Swanquarter.

Wetlands cover more than three-fourths of the county, and more than 90

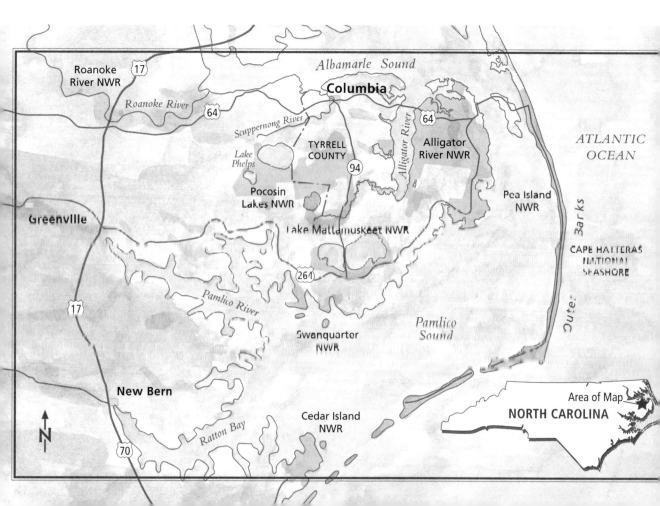

percent of the 260,000 acres in Tyrell is considered unbuildable.

Traditionally, the county economy drew on agriculture, forestry, and fishing. At the turn of the twentieth century, its waterfront and logging industry were vibrant. In the late 1980s, the threat of a proposed multicounty peat-mining operation at First Colony Farms brought together the commercial fishing industry and environmentalists, who fought and ultimately defeated it. Unable to mine peat, the owner tried to convert the forest for agricultural use by ditching, draining, and liming almost a thousand acres a week. The cost was prohibitive, and after a series of devastating underground wildfires in the drying peat, he went bankrupt.

People who had opposed the long-term environmental impacts of an extractive industry now became concerned about the hundreds of jobs lost when First Colony shut down and put the land on the market. A crisis had brought people together.

Vision 2000

In 1989, a national nonprofit organization, The Conservation Fund (TCF), acquired the 110,000-acre First Colony Farms at bankruptcy court. The combination of two factors—economic depression and the sale of the land to TCF—lies at the heart of what happened next.

A year before the purchase, Tyrrell County became one of twenty North Carolina communities chosen by the governor to receive assistance in promoting their coastal and coastal-plain resources. The Tyrrell County Coastal Initiative Committee had been formed to undertake comprehensive strategic planning to create Vision 2000, a plan intended to revitalize both town and county, and to improve the quality of life for all residents. Committee members included area businesspeople, town and county government officials, and grassroots leaders.

The committee evaluated a range of economic alternatives and surveyed residents regarding their preferences. The initial goal was to create a guide for redeveloping and revitalizing the waterfront in Columbia, the county seat.

Among other things, committee members wanted to show passersby—on average, five thousand cars per day, and more than 1.6 million tourists every year—what they were missing, and to entice them to stop. Yet, realistically, this idea had little chance of succeeding until the timing was right—until the people guiding it were prepared to encourage citizens of all racial and economic backgrounds to work together to achieve positive social and economic change and environmental protection. All in all, accomplishing the committee's goals would mean big changes in the way business was done in Tyrrell County.

The county has many historic sites, and the committee focused its plan on an approach that would, today, be labeled as "cultural" or "heritage" tourism. "The challenge is to revitalize and develop the waterfront in such a way that it appeals to both townspeople and visitors," the Vision 2000 committee concluded. "The town should be able to share both its present and its past . . . and not be something that it is not, just to attract tourists."

The committee listed additional needs, including productive and fulfilling jobs, a diverse tax base, and slowing "out migration" (people usually returned to the county only when retiring). Joint town-county ventures, it proposed, could help build a more effective infrastructure and encourage additional development while maintaining a relaxed, small-town atmosphere. Technical assistance could encourage local business opportunities and offer training to budding entrepreneurs. It suggested that the entire community focus on a single event, embracing *everyone*.

Partners

Tyrrell County administrator J.D. Brickhouse, an early and consistent supporter of Vision 2000, knows firsthand the importance of turning around the county's economy. Since beginning in 1970, he has worked on numerous projects to bring jobs to the area. So when The Conservation Fund's Dick Ludington came to talk with him about Vision 2000, Brickhouse was receptive to good economic-development ideas. By all accounts, his leadership has served as a cornerstone in the Vision 2000 process.

Carlisle Harrell was Columbia's town manager, recently retired, and an

original Vision 2000 participant. During his twenty-eight years on the job, he says, Tyrrell County has been "surveyed to death. Most results just sit on the shelf." The Coastal Communities Initiative and Vision 2000 changed everything, as county and town became partners for the first time. "At first," Harrell admits, "I thought this would be yet another dust gatherer." But this time, the combination of leadership and a good idea made all the difference, and beginning with the waterfront restoration project, the partners made steady progress. The county-town collaboration received a beach access grant in 1989, building 1,600 feet of boardwalk along the Scuppernong River. In 1990, more than 1,500 people helped dedicate it. "Impressive," Harrell says, "for a town of only nine hundred residents."

The Conservation Fund has had a North Carolina office in Chapel Hill since 1985. TCF offers a broad and innovative array of services to help North Carolina protect, enrich, and sustain its distinctive resources, whether natural, cultural, historic, economic, community, or human. The Fund's cornerstone Resourceful Communities Program focuses on helping local people achieve their own priorities (as in Vision 2000). TCF seeks to help them achieve those priorities within the context of environmental responsibility and longevity. They operate on the principle that rural residents are one of their greatest resources and are, in many cases, the true stewards of the land. This makes them eminently more qualified to decide on priorities. TCF then brings in their expertise to negotiate, help plan the work, or secure funding. This process makes for more "sustainable conservation" since there is local buy-in, and those who will carry it out for the long term are already in place in the community.

In 1989, when it purchased First Colony Farms at bankruptcy with funding from a private foundation, TCF began to work with Tyrrell County. Dick Ludington, then the Fund's southeast regional director, negotiated the real estate

The Resourceful Communities Program

The Resourceful Communities Program (RCP) of The Conservation Fund (TCF) is dedicated to empowering rural communities in North Carolina. Their mission is to involve a broad base of the community in creating new and just economies, and to ensure the long-term survival of their natural, cultural, and historic resources. The program began in the late 1990s with TCF's work in Tyrrell County, and grew to serve twenty-five of North Carolina's economically distressed, natural resource–rich counties. The program adapts old techniques to set new standards for how conservationists and economic developers can work together in rural communities.

The RCP works to help create new economies that protect and restore, rather than extract, natural resources in the poor, rural communities that are home to the state's most significant natural areas. This is particularly applicable to the Carolinas, where so much environmental degradation—such as the mining of coal and natural gas, and forest extraction—has been directly related to, and undertaken in the name of, "economic development."

Examples in North Carolina date back to the 1700s, when George Washington and his business partners tried to drain the Great Dismal Swamp to log it. In neighboring Hyde County, attempts to drain the 50,000-acre Lake Mattamuskeet for agricultural production established never-equaled yam production records, but ultimately resulted in bankruptcy for three companies. In western North Carolina, the old-growth forests were clear-cut, creating logging jobs that drew men from their farms but left them without employment or the skills needed for self-sufficiency when the timber companies closed down. More recently, First Colony Farms (see page 121) was originally slated for peat mining, subsequently turned toward large-scale agriculture, but ultimately went bankrupt because of high production costs, ecological instability, and large-scale wildfires caused by ditching and draining the peat wetlands.

Efforts to help local leaders address critical economic issues have resulted in a broad and inclusive collection of people working to protect the environment. This proactive approach also widens the prospect of available monies by channeling public and private funding for economic development, historic preservation, and social programs geared toward environmental protection.

The Resourceful Communities Program is grounded in TCF's vision of an enriched and just North Carolina. TCF sees a state made up of communities that respect and value both the diversity of and the connections between natural and human resources. They see a state where all individuals contribute to, and benefit from, fair and thoughtful decision-making. And they see economic and environmental interests working together to build strong communities.

TCF's Mikki Sager believes that their work has grown so much (although, she is quick to stress, the demand for their services far exceeds the time available) for several reasons. As she told me, "Given the geographic overlap of poverty and important natural areas, we have developed techniques that really work in economically distressed, natural resource–rich communities. To my knowledge, few other groups (especially national conservation groups) are doing this kind of work. The reason we are in such demand is because we produce results—jobs are created, organizations are strengthened, people are learning and growing, and proving every day that they don't have to choose between jobs and the environment. We have figured out how to help people do things without reinventing the wheel, and without needing million-dollar studies that will sit on the shelf. We have helped make the conservation movement *relevant* to rural realities, which is why people are comfortable with us."

And, as Mikki adds, "Time and again, people have been astounded that we don't seem to have an agenda (and we don't). If it's appropriate, we help them challenge the 'conventional wisdom' received from government agencies saying they must do things according to formulas developed in Raleigh or Washington, D.C. Most rural folks have been 'makin' do with what they've got' for many generations now, and the best way to continue is to build on their assets. We believe that rural folks are their own best asset.

"Because we help bring in money for our community partners, this helps them get important things done," Mikki continues. "By using conservation or environmental dollars to help address their own priorities, we are helping ensure that things are done in an environmentally responsible way—as most rural folks will do anyway. Rural folks accomplish amazing amounts of good with just a bit of funding. The best investment in land and natural resources is making sure they are in charge of what happens long-term in their communities."

deal, bringing his extensive experience and vision to bear and providing the "big picture" as to what was possible in Tyrrell County. Over the years Ludington held many strategic discussions with county and town officials, including Brickhouse, Harrell, and others about their ideas for revitalization. He also accompanied them on visits to Washington in search of funding and congressional support.

Ludington also trained Conservation Fund project managers Page Crutcher, a landscape architect, and Mikki Sager, a self-described generalist, encouraging them to think big, while remembering their conservation objectives and how to best integrate them. Using Crutcher's community-based design experience, the two adapted some of those elements to their efforts in Tyrrell County. Crutcher and Sager worked as a tag team, Crutcher focusing on developing a new greenway corridor, Sager on setting up a new community development corporation. They also developed bicycle trails for the Scuppernong River Greenway for several years until Crutcher moved to Seattle.

Sager, the strong, quietly encouraging force behind much of the collaborative process, majored in physical education in college. She also is a former world-class whitewater canoe racer. Most people don't believe her when she tells them about her education, thinking she must have advanced degrees in planning, environmental resources, or, at least, in community development. Starting as an administrative assistant at The Conservation Fund in 1990, she worked her way up by promoting the value of using a community-based focus. Until that time, TCF projects had tended toward land-based acquisitions and undertakings. Working initially with Crutcher, Sager needed to justify her intuition that by building coalitions through good relationships, they would best ensure success for the Tyrrell County Vision 2000 Initiative and TCF efforts that support and enhance it.

As she gained experience, Sager recalls, she noticed how rural communities consistently underestimate their abilities. She also saw outsiders trying to "fix" things without including locals in the process. Her leadership drew in people with a variety of skills and interests to help implement Vision 2000.

The respect for her is evident in the big smiles all kinds of people flash when they see her. She is direct, hardworking, thoughtful, accessible, and a lot of fun—qualities that go a long way in building the social framework necessary to accomplish the goal of improving community quality of life. "Generalists are the next step up the evolutionary ladder," she jokes, as if to reinforce her belief in her own abilities. To her, generalists are real people, doing real work with limited resources.

Piece by piece, the partners implemented elements of Vision 2000. The major components were the Pocosin Lakes National Wildlife Refuge (*Pocosin* is a Native American word for "swamp on a hill") and the Partnership for the Sounds, along with the restoration of the waterfront in Columbia.

The Pocosin Lakes National Wildlife Refuge comprises the former First Colony Farms (the 110,000 acres that were purchased by TCF in 1989). In 1990, TCF donated the refuge to the U.S. Fish & Wildlife Service. Today the refuge (now at 114,000 acres) serves as a critical piece in more than one million acres of ecologically sensitive habitat in the Albemarle-Pamlico Estuary. Recent statistics show 34,000 annual refuge visitors, and the figure is climbing. With an annual budget of $1.2 million, the refuge employs sixteen people.

By 1991, the town of Columbia and Tyrrell County were moving ahead with their plans. They joined forces to seek federal funds to build a "gateway" visitor center for Pocosin Lakes National Wildlife Refuge and the other six national wildlife refuges nearby, and to supplement funding from the North Carolina Department of Transportation for a rest area intended as an added incentive for tourists to stop as they passed through Tyrrell County.

The state's investment leveraged almost $5 million in federal and state appropriations, further supporting the development of facilities. First, the town and county partnered with the North Carolina Department of Transportation to establish a rest area facility and visitor center in Columbia on the Scuppernong

River. The facility houses the headquarters for the Partnership for the Sounds (PfS), the nonprofit organization that operates the visitor center. PfS was created in 1993 to promote "ecotourism" and environmental education as a regional economic development strategy in five of the most ecologically sensitive and economically distressed counties in eastern North Carolina. Tyrrell County administrator J.D. Brickhouse was founding board co-chair, and he continues to serve in that capacity.

These state investments then helped to leverage federal investment to construct the Walter B. Jones Center for the Sounds in Columbia (named for the late North Carolina congressman whose support was instrumental to these efforts). Through a unique public/private partnership, PfS linked the U.S. Fish & Wildlife Service's habitat conservation objectives with the environmentally responsible economic development goals of North Carolina and adjoining communities in neighboring states.

Tyrrell County, along with the North Carolina Department of Environment

Green Infrastructure

The following information about "green infrastructure" is taken from The Conservation Fund/USDA Forest Service Web site (see Resources for more).

What is Green Infrastructure?

Green Infrastructure is our nation's natural life support system —an interconnected network of protected land and water that supports native species, maintains natural ecological processes, sustains air and water resources, and contributes to the health and quality of life for America's communities and people.

Why Green Infrastructure?

Most land and water conservation initiatives in the United States are reactive, not proactive; haphazard, not systematic; piecemeal, not holistic; single scale, not multiscale; single purpose, not multifunctional. Current conservation efforts often focus on individual pieces of land, limiting their conservation benefits to the environment and human health. The mission of GreenInfrastructure.net is to illustrate that identifying and planning for Green Infrastructure—multipurpose green space networks—provides a framework for smart conservation and smart growth.

A city, county, or state would never build a road, water, or electrical system piece by piece, with no advanced planning or coordination between different system components and jurisdictions. These built infrastructure systems are planned, designed, and invested in far in advance of their actual use. We should plan, design, and invest in our Green Infrastructure following the same principles and approaches that are used for built infrastructure. A large coalition of public and private organizations is advancing the concept of Green Infrastructure nationwide.

and Natural Resources, played a leadership role in establishing PfS, setting standards for alternative approaches to job creation and small business development. PfS has since leveraged close to $20 million in state and federal funding to create a "green infrastructure" for ecotourism and environmental education in the region.

Some examples:

- The North Carolina Estuarium, "Where the Rivers Meet the Sea," in nearby "Little Washington" in Beaufort County, made possible with $4 million in state funding channeled through the North Carolina Department of Environment and Natural Resources, and $1 million from the local community;
- The historic Columbia Theater, renovated as a cultural museum, focusing on the areas of farming, fishing, forestry, and home life in Tyrrell County. The museum received a $10,000 grant from the Weyerhauser Corporation for the forestry exhibit;
- The rest area, visitor center, and the Walter B. Jones Center for the Sounds, headquarters for PfS in Columbia;
- Two buildings, recycled to serve as the Roanoke River National Wildlife Refuge Headquarters and a PfS environmental education center in the Roanoke/Cashie River Center in Bertie County;
- Renovations to the historic Mattamuskeet Lodge at Lake Mattamuskeet National Wildlife Refuge in Hyde County;
- A $100,000 boardwalk built with help from the Eckerd Family Foundation, including 3,200 feet of interpretive boardwalk and wildlife overlooks built by the Tyrrell County Youth Conservation Corps (see below) and interpretive signage installed by the Partnership for the Sounds; and
- Planning for a Red Wolf Sanctuary in Tyrrell County, harboring the indigenous red wolf, which exists in the wild today only in the PfS area, to be built by the Red Wolf Coalition.

In 1995, the Walter B. Jones Center for the Sounds was completed. In addition to housing the Pocosin Lakes National Wildlife Refuge Visitor Center and a Partnership for the Sounds office, it also serves as the headquarters for the twenty-seven-mile-long Scuppernong River Greenway, and offers an outdoor classroom built by the partnership and given to the refuge.

A number of features, including the mile-long interpretive boardwalk, have made this one of the most visited facilities in North Carolina. The center's

traditional eastern North Carolina architecture, complete with rocking chairs and a wraparound porch, welcomes visitors to share the community's present and past, as prescribed in the original Vision 2000 plan. Whereas most people used to drive by on their way east, now many stop to rest, take a look at the visitor center, and often go into downtown Columbia. Mikki Sager claims merchants there have noticed a marked increase in purchases by visitors. The evidence is anecdotal but reliable, she says; "When you live in small town, you always know when an outsider walks in."

Community Development

To complement the environmental, tourism, and economic development–oriented projects underway, the Tyrrell County Community Development Corporation (CDC) was formed in 1992 to help minorities with promising business ideas get started, providing technical assistance, business management help, and information. To ensure equal representation at the table, and after lengthy and sometimes heated discussion, the composition of the first CDC board of directors became 50 percent white and 50 percent black. According to several accounts, this decision became a watershed experience for the community. Board policy also called for a three-quarters-majority vote to approve proposals and outcomes. To validate them, three-quarters of the directors needed to attend meetings. At the time this hard-fought board by-law represented a true milestone, resulting in the first racially balanced CDC in North Carolina.

The founding board president was a soulful and visionary man named Henry Hill who served in that capacity for ten years. By all accounts, Mr. Henry Hill (as he's known to everyone) provided thoughtful and steady leadership to the CDC in all that time. He recalled for me that, when he began, access for minorities to such simple amenities as fax machines, copiers, and the Internet was difficult to come by. The CDC provided those services and offered professional

"By focusing initial efforts on creating opportunities for the county's young people, Mavis was able to generate strong support among adult community leaders for natural resource protection and sustainable economic activities."

counseling for creating business plans and presentations, and giving access to loan pools.

After receiving funding to support the CDC start-up, The Conservation Fund was given a seat on the board. TCF also provided initial staff support to the CDC before transferring responsibilities to the first staff person, Mavis Hill. Mavis Hill is a single mother and ball of fire who began as volunteer CDC board secretary, serving as both officer and "do-it-all" administrator. When a search was launched to hire the first executive director, Henry Hill (no relation) supported her for that position. He felt Mavis possessed many qualities necessary for guiding the fledgling nonprofit to new levels.

After working together closely for several years, The Conservation Fund's Mikki Sager says that Mavis Hill was one real key to shifting the ways in which people of all races worked together in Tyrrell County. "She was both young and wise beyond her years—an important combination that helped so much because she could see the possibilities and figure out how to make things happen to challenge the status quo while helping people feel less intimidated about her actions." And, Sager adds, "By focusing initial efforts on creating opportunities for the county's young people, Mavis was able to generate strong support among adult community leaders for natural resource protection and sustainable economic activities. This resonated for African-American community leaders because natural resource–based projects and programs provide job training and career opportunities—and a future—for the county's young adults."

Mavis Hill's success was such that, in 1998, she received the American Land Conservation Award, accompanied by a check for $50,000, at the national Land Trust Alliance Rally in Madison, Wisconsin, with over 1,200 colleagues in attendance. Sager recalls, "For once, Mavis Hill was speechless!" As a result of her accomplishments, Hill sits on a number of boards and committees across the state, a prime example of learning by doing.

Doris Maldonado came to the CDC about five years ago, looking for help with a business plan. She lives in nearby Alligator, an unincorporated community of 350 people, mostly African-American, many living at or below the poverty level. At the time the community desperately needed new leadership to move forward. "One night," Maldonado recalls, "I went to an Alligator Community Association meeting and came home as president."

She acknowledges the good that has come to her community from both the

BELOW: The visitor center headquarters informs passersby about the abundance of natural resources in Tyrrell County.

CDC and the Tyrrell County Vision 2000 initiative. In fact, Alligator will soon have its first Neighborhood Watch—the first such community-led program in the county for deterring crime. In addition, the Alligator Community Association is working to implement small businesses and ecotourism programs near the Little Alligator River at the Palmetto-Peartree Preserve, on land bought by The Conservation Fund. Maldonado gives much credit to the Fund for spearheading meaningful projects that boost community efforts.

Michael Harrell joined the CDC in 1999 as director of the Northeastern North Carolina Black Chamber of Commerce, representing sixteen counties. Based on an established national model, his organization seeks to be "the voice of black people wanting to build small businesses," he explains. Though he initially called Mavis Hill about helping with the CDC steering committee, he soon became an integral member of the organization. Harrell notes with pride that the "Tyrrell County Community Development Corporation is recognized for its ability to be there." According to him, many CDCs formerly focused mainly on *buildings*, but in a recent positive move, they have shifted toward helping *people* to empower themselves. To him, the Tyrrell County CDC is a leader in providing new models for rural development in North Carolina.

One such model is the Regional Enterprise Incubator Network, a small-business incubator operated by the CDC. Unlike urban incubators providing low-cost space for new businesses, the Tyrrell version provides planning, financial, administrative, and technical assistance to help start up enterprises through the first three to five years. The thirty-six minority owned businesses served by this program credit the incubator with providing stability and access to loans. All Incubator clients strive to be environmentally responsible in their actions.

The Tyrrell County Youth Conservation Corps is another such model. Under the direction of the CDC since 1993, the Youth Conservation Corps has provided job skills and educational training for young adults from seventeen to twenty-five years of age. Modeled after the Civilian Conservation Corps of the 1930s Great Depression era, Youth Corps internships offer hands-on training and work experience with state and federal conservation agencies through conservation career–based internships. The corps makeup consists of 75 percent minorities and 50 percent females. The four-day work week comprises job and physical skills training with a focus on teamwork, responsibility, community service, and a good work ethic. The fifth day incorporates education—the goal is for each member to complete a high school diploma or GED, or to start college courses. The overall program goal is to place each member in a full-time, permanent job or to continue at a school of higher learning. Since being founded, the corps has enrolled more than 150 youth in training programs.

Twenty-five-year-old Tracy Spruill is a former Youth Corps member. With a hunger to learn new things, Tracy was interested when he first heard about the CDC and the Corps. The CDC staff sometimes literally plucked kids off street corners as participants, and Tracy was one of them. As Henry Hill notes, "Many kids just nodded or grunted when spoken to when they first started. But by the time they finished the program, they actually talked." Tracy went two rounds with the Corps, becoming a supervisor the second time. He went on to work at the historic Somerset Place Plantation. When the manager saw he was a conscientious and hard worker, she called the CDC and asked specifically for him. As Michael Harrell suggests, such landscaping skills and others developed through the Youth Corps can lead to future business possibilities for their members.

Since its inception, the CDC has proven to be a real asset to the community. As Mavis Hill notes, the organization helps, on average, between six to ten businesses a year get started and, no doubt, inspires countless other ideas for future reference. Now those ideas have a much better chance of becoming reality.

Ten Thousand Visitors

Vision 2000 has spawned a number of other successful projects. One of the most popular elements of the plan was the idea of creating a single, community-wide event that would embrace everyone. This notion bore fruit in 1991 when the town and county partnership launched a new waterfront festival in Columbia designed to celebrate the entire community and to draw in visitors. Since 1991 the Scuppernong River Festival has been held the second Saturday of October, regularly attracting ten thousand people. (The town has less than a thousand residents!) A daylong, family-oriented affair, the Festival offers music, a stage, an antique car show, pontoon boat rides, dancing, art shows, fireworks, and a perennial favorite—an Elvis act. The River Festival has, in fact, become so integrated into community life that people have begun scheduling family and class reunions around that weekend. As former town manager Carlisle Harrell told me, "I knew we had a hit when someone I grew up with told me this reminded him of the way Columbia used to be on a Saturday night." The festival unites the community in a big way, Harrell said. "It draws from afar and it brings people home." The food and music are great, but it's really all about people and relationships. As county administrator J.D. Brickhouse notes, "You see more people hugging and kissing than anything else."

Another program, the Scuppernong River Greenway project, began in 1994

Somerset Place

Somerset Place is a representative antebellum plantation offering an insightful view of life during the period before the Civil War. During its eighty-year existence as an active plantation (1786–1865), it encompassed as many as one hundred thousand acres and became one of North Carolina's most prosperous rice, corn, and wheat plantations. It was home to more than three hundred enslaved men, women, and children of African descent, eighty of whom were brought to Somerset directly from their West African homeland in 1786. These were people who had firsthand knowledge of rice cultivation. Slaves dug a system of irrigation and transportation canals; built a sawmill, gristmills, barns, stables, work buildings, and dwelling houses; and cultivated fields.

According to Mikki Sager of The Conservation Fund, Somerset is significant for several reasons. It is one of the sites that started doing "heritage tourism" before anyone had coined the term. Site manager Dorothy Spruill Redford was responsible for changing the focus of the interpretive programs there. A descendant of slaves who worked at Somerset, she wanted people to learn about her history and the history of slavery. When visiting, you will hear about the Collins family that lived in the big house, but most of the interpretation focuses on the lives of the slaves. Dorothy was one of the first people in the country to offer that type of interpretation. She also created a special Homecoming Celebration every two years, bringing slave descendants back to Somerset. Families come by the busload to the Homecoming, and it has become a real celebration of their African roots. Both the plantation and the Homecoming Celebration are a big boost to Tyrrell County's focus on ecotourism and heritage tourism. As Mikki observes, the relationship has been largely positive because Somerset is a full partner with the CDC and the Youth Corps and has helped round out the Corps members' experiences a great deal.

CONFERENCE CENTER

with The Conservation Fund's purchase of eight hundred acres along the river.
A twenty-seven-mile network of canoe and pedestrian trails will link the river,
Pocosin Lakes National Wildlife Refuge and Visitor Center, and the waterfront
of Columbia, to the Somerset Place plantation on Lake Phelps. At this point the
Greenway is partially in place, with boardwalks, a couple of canoe platforms,
and several trails built. Interestingly, this project has provided the foundation
for a proposed state park, so construction is occurring in pieces. A number of
canoe access points and platforms have been developed by the Partnership for
the Sounds, and the Tyrrell County CDC is working to identify potential rental
businesses and guide services.

Another component is the Palmetto-Peartree Preserve, created in 1999 when
The Conservation Fund purchased 9,732 acres along Albemarle Sound. Funding came from the North Carolina Department of Transportation endangered
species mitigation program, offsetting habitat loss due to road construction in
nearby areas. The preserve contains a mixture of hardwood swamp, hardwood
and pine forest, and marsh. The project will serve as a model for red-cockaded
woodpecker habitat management, sustainable forestry, and sustainable ecotourism
development in rural communities. The ultimate goal is to attract bird-watchers
and ecotourists, and to support the development of related small, locally owned
businesses. To date, three interpretive trails and a half-mile boardwalk offer bird
watching and natural history lessons for visitors.

The Eastern 4-H Environmental Conference Center, also a Vision 2000 project, opened in May of 2001. Although relatively new, the Center draws from
a wide geographic area. It offers an agricultural focus, including a 4-H youth
department and a cooperative extension program. The Center exists to provide
a forum for community interaction; groups may reserve the facility for retreats,
weddings, family functions, and civic and social gatherings. Offerings include
learning weekends, summer camps, and programs for underserved children. An

interpretive boardwalk through the forest and a swimming pool are other recent and popular additions. Challenging ropes courses have been designed as character-building exercises for youth and to teach leadership and team-building skills to corporate executives.

The Center was paid for by the North Carolina General Assembly and is owned by the state. The Conservation Fund helped to secure land acquisition funding for the facility in the early 1990s. Although the decision to locate in Tyrrell County was hotly debated at first, the scenic site on the banks of Albemarle Sound has proven successful. Sara Phelps, sales and marketing manager, is responsible for promoting the Center's amenities to both Tyrrell County and surrounding counties. She says that the response to the facility, both locally and regionally, has been phenomenal. In explanation she says simply, "The 4-H Center reflects the notion that our everyday life and our community does matter."

The Arts

The implementation of Vision 2000 was further enhanced in 1994 when former art teacher Feather Phillips, recognizing the importance of connecting culture to environment through the arts (see Chapter 7, *Hand in Hand*, on page 171), founded Pocosin Arts. When the Vision 2000 plan surfaced, Phillips noticed how it met many of her personal objectives, and she wanted to be at the table. In a stroke of good timing, Phillips and Pocosin Arts stepped into a pronounced gap; while several excellent community arts organizations existed in the state, they were located eight or nine hours away in western North Carolina.

Early on, Pocosin Arts initiated a unique pilot program, "locking" scientists and artists together in one room with the goal of discovering common experiences, to give people a better sense of themselves and their artistic talents. Environmental educators learned they were already creative in their existing work, which usually went beyond curriculum guides by engaging students experientially in the natural world.

In a stroke of good timing, Phillips and Pocosin Arts stepped into a pronounced gap; while several excellent community arts organizations existed in the state, they were located eight or nine hours away in western North Carolina.

At Pocosin Arts, taking the artistic process and making it one's own is encouraged. Phillips remembers one educator at the initial session, who had never created anything. "After the woman made her first pot, she was literally transformed by the experience," she says. Program participants used locally dug clay and became inspired by the archaeological forms and designs viewed in a slide presentation on early Native American pot forms and traditions, as well as "hand-of-the artist" designs such as leaves or twigs, impressed on fabric. For its part, Phillips adds, this group learned the important lesson that every human being has the capacity to be both an artist and a scientist, and is not limited to a single label or job description.

The pilot program's success gave the organization the impetus to seek funding for a new initiative, Connecting Culture to the Environment through the Arts. The goal was to help the community to know itself and each other through music, stories, and art. In the ensuing years, Pocosin Arts established a gallery, a gift shop, and workshop/studio space for artists to take classes and to create and sell their work. The complex has become a local gathering point for local and regional artists to share creative ideas and skills, and an added attraction for visitors to Columbia and Tyrrell County.

As the recent millenium drew near, Pocosin Arts searched for a unique project to commemorate it. Phillips particularly admired a signature piece by German conceptual artist Joseph Beuys, who began as a scientist specializing in social sculpture. When Beuys returned to a war-ravaged Germany after serving as a fighter pilot in World War II, he witnessed the horrific physical and psychological damage to his country. The experience profoundly shifted his focus from science toward art, and toward art that would engage the spirit and speak to community. Beuys's exhibit, entitled "7,000 Oaks," planted in Germany in the 1980s, provided the inspiration for a Tyrrell County installation called "7,000 Juniper." Pocosin Arts partnered with several professors at the Art School at East Carolina University in Greenville on the design. After being heavily logged during the first part of the twentieth century, the junipers—known also as Atlantic white cedar—did not grow back in North Carolina. The 7,000 Juniper project was created for the dual purpose of drawing attention to the plight of the trees and serving as a restoration effort. It sits on land purchased by The Conservation Fund with National Fish & Wildlife Foundation funding, and later transferred to the Pocosin Lakes National Wildlife Refuge.

The planning and planting process involved U.S. Fish & Wildlife Service staff, scientists, artists, and educators from the University of North Carolina at Chapel Hill and North Carolina State. Project elements include creating a demonstration forest, learning about forestry, archaeology, and creativity, and discovering the spiritual benefits of helping to preserve these endangered trees. Trees were planted in groupings each year (in Beuys's case, it took five years to plant all the trees). A special 7,000 Juniper Millenium marker has been placed under each tree in honor or memory of someone chosen by each donor. The last planting took place on April 7, 2004. The forest is fast becoming a sacred place of remembrance.

As did Beuys, Phillips and Pocosin Arts hope to involve people in solving problems in positive and creative ways. Children participate in the 7,000 Juniper project by creating clay markers and objects, and burying them beneath the trees. Feather feels they are leaving parts of their spirits in the ground and will, she hopes, come away with a newly instilled responsibility for the future. Through this and other offerings, Pocosin Arts and its supporters serve as a wonderful complement to the Vision 2000 plan in Tyrrell County and beyond.

Connecting
CULTURE
to
ENVIRONMENT
through the **ARTS**

POCOSIN ARTS
Main and Water streets
Columbia, North Carolina

On the picturesque Scuppernong River

Secrets

The benefits of Vision 2000 clearly have begun to ripple outward. Just before I finished writing this story, TCF's Mikki Sager relayed the exciting news that a collaborative effort on entrepreneurship in the five-county Partnership for the Sounds area was recently funded with a community development block grant of $100,000. Tyrrell County was the applicant, partnering with the CDC, the Partnership for the Sounds, the Eastern 4-H Center, and The Conservation Fund on natural resource–based, small business development. Components will include outreach and educational workshops, ongoing technical assistance, leadership development courses, and a manual with standardized information on ecosystems and environmental tourism—all of which will comprise a rural, grassroots MBA-like program for budding entrepreneurs.

What are the secrets behind Vision 2000's success? "Basically, the initiative was accomplished with common sense and resourcefulness, exactly what is needed—and found—in rural communities," Mikki Sager asserts. She lists the factors that led to success:

- Addressing challenging issues internally (otherwise people would never have to deal with them);
- Addressing the economic distress and social disparity found in each community;
- Understanding how people see threats to their environment or their ability to make a living;
- Creating a new model for successful collaboration, using local resources to the utmost;
- Planting seeds for civic engagement: in this case, local leaders fully supported the process, going beyond the usual steps by speaking with many more black professionals than ever before during the survey phase;
- Creating the right atmosphere by giving people a chance to participate who never had before, and thereby expanding the pool of engaged citizens;
- Broadening the base of county leadership;
- Offering a broader definition of what constitutes economic development;
- Creating new jobs in a county that hadn't seen them in a very long time and that desperately needed them;
- Connecting traditional economics with traditional environmentalism by tying together all actions to protecting the environment and making that notion relevant to everyone in the community, including people of color, and those living in poverty; and
- Improving the environment in general; of the county's 260,000 acres, 90,227 are now in conservation.

For those of us who show up to help improve the quality of life in any community, we would do well to remember that it already is home to those who live there. This advice speaks to the importance of creating meaningful partnerships between those who reside in and care about a place, regardless of the length of time, or how their perspectives differ. Even if plans are implemented properly, they will take time to come to fruition. This work requires an investment of time and energy, not to mention funding, and the understanding that the richness lies in the journey to achieve the vision. In the process, the many small steps will add up to one large leap, positively changing the way people of all walks of life relate to themselves and to each other.

By having the courage to embrace new ways of thinking about the environment as it relates to the economies of Columbia and Tyrrell County, the people involved in Vision 2000 began a process that can lead them into the future. Their plan provides visitors with new opportunities to pause and experience the county's scenic natural areas. Interpretive exhibits—and places to walk, rest, and appreciate—give visitors a better understanding of the diverse talents and interests of people across the county. The acts of creating the Scuppernong River Festival and an innovative arts program, restoring buildings and the waterfront, and offering multiple resources to support traditionally underserved minorities have enriched and renewed the community. To those who live there and others who only visit, the benefits are already beyond measure.

"When you remember who you are, and how you are connected, you build from the in-side out." —Alexie Torres-Fleming, Bronx native, executive director of Youth Ministries for Peace and Justice, Bronx River Alliance member

6

THE BRONX RIVER PROJECT

The Bronx, New York—*Community residents and other partners in one of the country's most economically challenged urban areas find success—and themselves—through the process of restoring their river.*

This is a story about people, many from humble origins, who became empowered and transformed by working together on a vast, and oftentimes seemingly unachievable goal: cleaning up New York City's Bronx River. Although a number of noble efforts undertaken over several decades began to revitalize the river, none captured the attention of Bronx residents sufficiently to convince them to join in to help. Therefore, the project languished. Indeed, this is not surprising, for how could anyone have much hope when the message he or she hears from childhood is that home is a dumping ground?

When I visited the Bronx River Project over a period of several years and listened to some of the people involved, I was surprised by how strongly that perception dominates their consciousness. So it was all the more striking to hear the stories of how these people reached inside themselves to find strengths they never dreamed they had. And to see how residents became engaged in the project this time, and, finally, to witness their evolution from bystanders, to participants, to community leaders.

The people in this story were instrumental in helping to turn the project toward success, yet they represent only a few of those involved in total. Indeed, I learned about the sheer numbers of people necessary, working together, before they can make even a small difference in urban areas. And, ironically, how those closest to a resource sometimes require a catalyst to spark their interest in preserving it. Such was the role of the Bronx River Project.

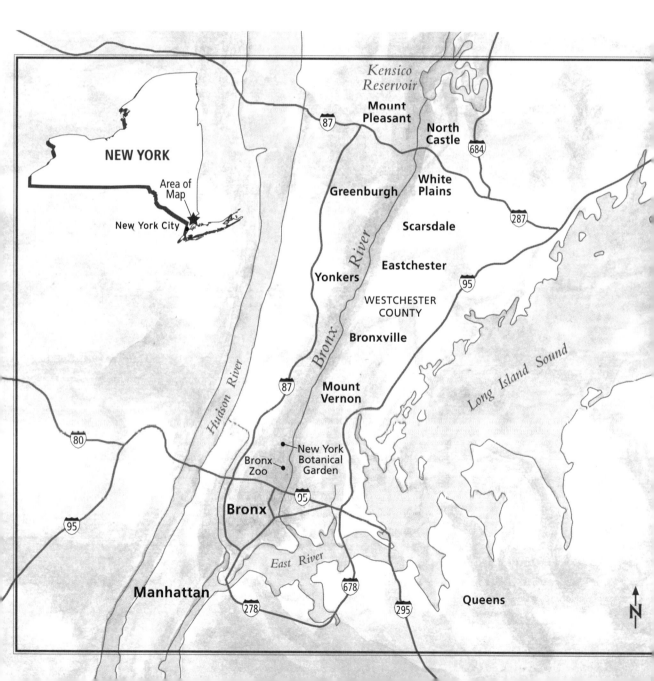

Majora Carter and Alexie Torres-Fleming grew up just blocks from the Bronx River, but they didn't even know it existed. In many places mounds of scrap metal or other junk more than twenty feet high obscured the view. The direction of their lives changed forever when the community began to organize around revitalizing and reclaiming their river, and they joined in the effort.

The Bronx River flows twenty-three miles from suburban Westchester County, through the heart of the Bronx, on its way to the East River and Long Island Sound. It passes from one of the wealthiest counties in the country to one of the poorest. It travels through two counties, four towns, four cities, three villages, five New York City council districts, and four congressional districts. According to U.S. Census 2000 data, Congressional District #16 in the Bronx has a poverty rate of 40.2 percent—the highest in the country. With a population of 1.3 million, the Bronx also has the nation's lowest median household income, at $27,611.

As the river passes through the Bronx it is fragmented, crossed by railroads, four highways, and "islands" of heavy industry. Garbage streams into the river from streets and storm drains. Combined sewer overflows pour raw sewage into the river whenever it rains heavily and, until recently, illegal dumping went completely unchecked. For much of the twentieth century, the river was hidden and forgotten, having been seriously fouled in the nineteenth century by industrial waste.

Yet, all along, certain attributes of the Bronx River have held promise for improvement. Until it meets the tidal section just below the Bronx Zoo, it is the only freshwater river in New York City. It bisects more than nine hundred acres of open space. And despite the pollution, the river contains beautiful "pocket" landscapes and a variety of birds, plants, and animals.

Such glimpses of naturalness and the desire to reclaim the river led to an initial Bronx River cleanup in 1974. But not until 1996 did the concept of a citizen effort register more broadly in the hearts and minds of Bronx residents.

At that time, the Bronx RiverKeeper Program was the vehicle, created to train volunteers as water-quality monitors of the river's biological health, in partnership with Consolidated Edison and the City of New York Parks and Recreation Department. This program marked the start of greater community engagement in the Bronx River's well-being.

Then in 1997 the National Park Service Rivers & Trails Program and the Appalachian Mountain Club (AMC) teamed up with the New York City–based program, Partnerships for Parks, to begin collective, strategic river improvement. Partnerships for Parks hired a Bronx River Coordinator, who led the

Art as Expression of Self, Community, and Environmental Value

When I visited with Majora Carter, more than a dozen pieces of art lined the walls of the Sustainable South Bronx office, made from such junk as battered car doors, hubcaps, car windows, and other found objects. Painted or pasted onto them were powerful poems and reflections by people living in the South Bronx and in Durban, South Africa—the result of a cultural exchange in which people in both places gave voice to surprisingly similar feelings about their longings and frustrations. These works of art offer people from outside the neighborhood—sometimes *way* outside—a compelling sense of how it feels to reclaim community pride from desperate circumstances.

Art can be a vitally important aspect of any restoration effort. Here it was used as a universal language and springboard for raising community consciousness. In 1999 the Working Group initiated a special event around the Golden Ball—a 36-inch gold-painted plastic sphere symbolizing the "sun, energy and spirit of the river." Conveyed downriver by volunteers in canoes, the ball and the accompanying festivities invited residents to the river, uniting the communities through which it passed, unobstructed. The Golden Ball served as a visible and effective tool for communicating that point because it did not change shape or size as it floated down the river—the communities did. Conceived through the National Park Service Art & Community Landscapes initiative, this project was, and still is, a big hit—with residents, businesses, politicians, and the media—so much so that it is staged annually. Celebratory events such as nature walks, bike rides, river cleanups, games, and music draw people of all ages to the river. (See Chapter 7, *Hand in Hand*, and Resources for more information.)

project and eventually convened the Bronx River Working Group. (Partnerships for Parks is a joint initiative of the New York City Department of Parks & Recreation and the nonprofit City Parks Foundation; AMC is a nonprofit conservation organization founded in 1876 to protect the woodlands, mountains, rivers, and trails in the Appalachian region from Maine to Virginia—see Resources.) This time, more than forty partners got involved, including government agencies, nonprofit institutions, schools, scientists, businesses, and community groups. The partners also realized the need to embrace *all* people living near the river, whether or not they even knew it existed. Soon the Working Group extended its reach to include more than sixty community organizations, schools, businesses, and government agencies, a number that eventually reached more than seventy-five.

Collaboration

Like many underserved communities, the Bronx is full of "outside experts" wanting to help improve the standard of living. These could be scientists, planners, or people associated with social service agencies, with good intentions but with a regional or

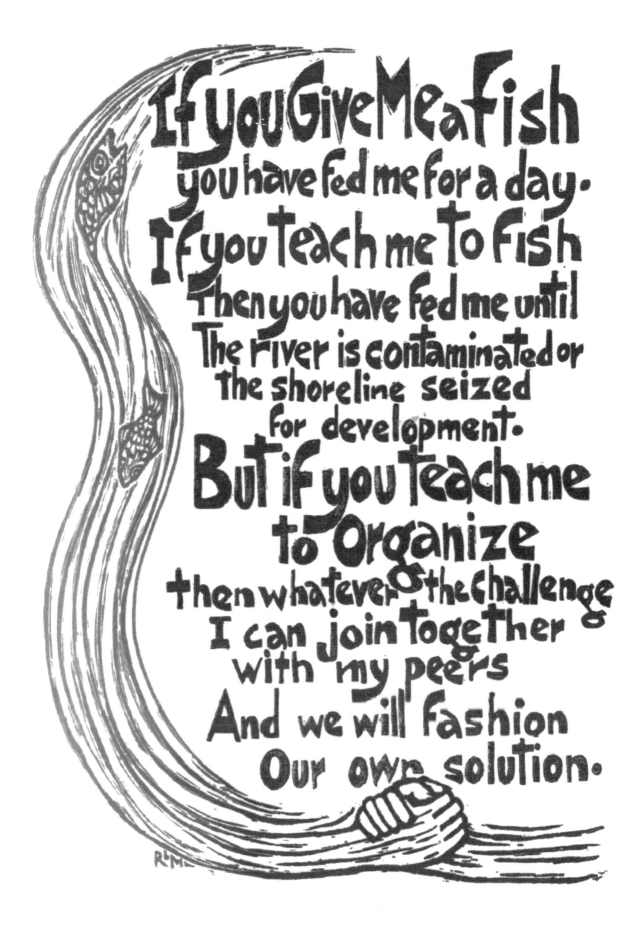

If you Give Me a fish
you have fed me for a day.
If you teach me to fish
then you have fed me until
the river is contaminated or
the shoreline seized
for development.
But if you teach me
to Organize
then whatever the challenge
I can join together
with my peers
And we will fashion
Our own solution.

national orientation. Inevitably, though, the impetus for any major social change must come from within. Residents, in reality, are the experts by virtue of living there.

Collaborative strategies proved to be pivotal in moving the restoration effort forward and in sparking a shift in attitude on the part of Bronx residents. Fortunately, a new generation of community activists has emerged who have learned these lessons and skills firsthand.

The Bronx River coordinator hired by Partnerships for Parks was Jenny Hoffner, an energetic and thoughtful young woman characteristically modest about her contributions to the restoration effort. This very quality made her a good choice to facilitate the process. Her collaborative leadership experience was limited when she was chosen as the first Working Group coordinator, so she relied on her instincts, initially spending time listening to people's dreams for the river. How would it look and be used? Who, ideally, would visit?

In the early days, Hoffner recalls, members of the Working Group possessed lots of ideas and tried many tactics, some of which worked while others didn't. Successes included creating a colorful river map and guide, and hosting numerous art events, cleanups, and a boating flotilla along the length of the river. A forest inventory project to determine the number and species of trees along the river was less successful because of bad timing and lack of funding. Hoffner is confident, however, that the general concept remains sound. "Someone just has to fall in love with the forest," she says. "Then this project will get done, too."

Another instrumental Working Group member is Dart Westphal, a fifty-year-old veteran historic preservationist and environmental activist who came to the area by way of his master's thesis on community gardening in the South Bronx.

He studied at the Institute for Local Self-Reliance (see Resources). Since 1974, the Institute has worked with citizen groups, governments, and private businesses in developing policies that extract the maximum value from local resources.

Westphal and his family live in the Bronx. Currently he serves as executive director of Mosholu Preservation Corporation, a nonprofit organization created in 1981 by Montefiore Medical Center in response to the difficulty of attracting qualified health-care professionals to its hospital. Mosholu's mission is to preserve and revitalize the Reservoir Oval neighborhood surrounding the hospital, creating a better place for staff to live and work. Over the past few decades, Mosholu has rehabilitated numerous residential and commercial buildings, parks, and monuments. An abandoned reservoir became a park, with a sea of daffodils blooming there each spring. Westphal joined the Bronx River Working Group with a keen eye toward complementing the work of his organization.

Westphal knows from experience the importance of perseverance and timing. "It's been a long restoration process," he says. "Plus, when an economic boom hits New York City, by the time it reaches the Bronx, the boom has likely crashed. This has happened five times already in my experience. If you are in a disfavored place like the Bronx, you'll always be last in line."

He remains cautious about the progress, knowing too well how things such as lawsuits over contamination can delay or defeat good projects. "Something can get stopped and never come back," he says. "If you miss your moment, your moment can pass. You have to be ready. You have to be first in line."

Local Leaders Emerge

As members of the Working Group gained experience, they began to focus on achieving goals for going forward, including raising the project visibility, engaging community members of all ages, identifying complementary partners, and assigning distinct roles for them to assume. One key player in this process was an insightful young woman from a Hispanic-American neighborhood.

Alexie Torres-Fleming wasn't much concerned with the environment growing up; she was busy just surviving. Home for her was the Bronx River projects,

BRONX
RIVER

ALLIANCE

"If you miss your moment, your moment can pass. You have to be ready. You have to be first in line."

yet, like Majora Carter, the debris and the built environment kept her from realizing that the river for which the buildings were named flowed nearby. Like other neighborhood children, she learned from an early age to cling to the familiar mantra: "I will be successful when I can escape from here."

Although she left the Bronx for a time to pursue college degrees and other interests, she ultimately returned, drawn to making a meaningful contribution to her community. "I come to this work from a sacred place, especially through the act of rebuilding and restoring the river," Torres-Fleming says. She notes with gratitude the positive effect the project has had on the neighborhood's sense of spirituality and community, in direct contrast to the sometimes angry, oppressed sentiments she was used to hearing expressed about her home while growing up, especially concerning the hopelessness of life in the Bronx.

For Torres-Fleming, a pivotal experience came in 1992 when a neighborhood church was suddenly torched one night. In response, some 1,200 outraged people marched in protest, many of them community members who, until then, considered themselves powerless, including her own father. Later, she says, she realized that part of the reason for this and other acts of vandalism lay with the lack of services available for young people. Diversions such as sports and arts existed, but they were not designed "to reach the roots of their souls," as she calls it. Wanting to somehow reconnect to her community, she founded the nonprofit

ABOVE: If one looks carefully, one can find beauty in both obvious and subtle places along the river.
RIGHT: The NYC Parks Department's Natural Resources Group created a saltwater plant nursery (still in use) on the grounds of the old concrete plant, to nurture saltmarsh grasses and other plants used in restoring the river banks.

Youth Ministries for Peace and Justice to help channel young people's energy. The program utilized art and education as powerful tools of expression, not merely as entertainment. As part of their mission, Youth Ministries taught the value not only of individual success, but also of selflessness, collective work, and concern for one's neighbors.

Youth Ministries joined the Bronx River Working Group as a way of engaging kids of all ages through direct experience in making a difference. To give them greater perspective, staff members drove the Youth Ministries kids fifteen minutes north to view the river as it flowed through affluent, suburban Bronxville. Observing the abundance of birds and animals upriver, they asked, "Why is it so nice here and not so nice where *we* live?" To them, Bronx parks were not real—they were made of concrete.

The experience sowed the seeds of the kids' determination to improve river conditions downstream from the Bronx Zoo and the New York Botanical Garden. Restoration efforts had not yet reached south beyond those two landmark institutions.

Youth Ministries created the team it called RIVER (Reaching & Including youth Voices for Environmental Rights). These thirteen- to twenty-one-year-olds committed themselves collectively to "the environmental healing of our community." Younger participants, aged eight to twelve, were called the River Friends. As a result of the work of both RIVER groups, more than forty cars, ten thousand tires, and countless other items were pulled from the river. The effort didn't just clean the river; it also invigorated the young volunteers. As one RIVER team member put it, "This project has allowed me to see that the Bronx River represents *us*, the people who live in the Bronx. We *can* make a difference!"

Youth Ministries also created Project ROW (Reclaim Our Waterfront), complementing the agenda of the Bronx River Working Group. Initiatives included

restoring the river to a cleaner state, replanting ten acres at a former cement factory, decommissioning the Sheridan Expressway to create a park, reclaiming the long-neglected Starlight Park (site of a former gas plant that had been contaminated and unused since 1912), and building a network of trails Youth Ministries also created an "anti-displacement campaign" to ensure that low- and middle-income families could continue to afford to live there once economic and environmental conditions improved.

Most important, Youth Ministries trained its members in the finer points of community organizing, strategizing, and identifying key "players" to approach for help. Potential partners included city, state, and federal governments, the Environmental Protection Agency, the New York State Department of Environmental Conservation, Westchester County government, the New York Department of Transportation, and the state office of parks.

Bronx River Watershed Education Program

Bronx River Stewards. Each year two workshops train teachers and community educators to monitor river conditions. They collect water-quality data, monitor flora and fauna living in the watershed, and report incidents of pollution to the Alliance, working in conjunction with area scientists to ensure the accuracy of the data gathering.

Bronx River Classroom. As living laboratories, the river and its watershed serve as the basis for lesson plans, bringing the river to the classroom and the classroom to the river. Lessons include water-quality analysis, macroinvertebrate analysis, "Environment in the Community," "Plants in the City," and "What is a Watershed?"

Public Education and Outreach. Canoe tours, both recreational and educational, offer the public a new perspective on the river and its value to the community. Groups such as the AMC, Rocking the Boat (a nonprofit organization that teaches students to build small wooden boats for use on the river), Youth Ministries for Peace and Justice, Mosholu Preservation

Corporation, and the Urban Park Rangers work together to create more opportunities for community participation.

It wasn't all work. Youth Ministries engaged its members in a variety of activities, including the Amazing Bronx River Flotilla, a popular community-wide celebration now in its sixth year, sponsored by the Working Group partners. In anticipation of this event, several canoes were purchased. As the kids carried them on their heads through the urban streets to launch them, several astonished onlookers asked, "What are those things and what are you doing with them?"

Alexie Torres-Fleming, reflecting on her participation, says she's gained a feeling of solidarity with her community—which has, in turn, been educated through her efforts. She views her ability as a leader to help envision a better future as "a sacred responsibility." Still, she realizes she's not always the expert, and has learned to rely on others. The experience has instilled in her tremendous hope for possibilities in the world, at the same time opening up the world to her. "People have reclaimed not only the river but also something deep inside of them," she says. "When you remember who you are, and how you are connected, you build from the inside out."

When Jenny Hoffner first called Majora Carter, another member of the Bronx River Working Group, to ask for her assistance in energizing and activating members of her African-American community, and in finding options for a seed grant of $10,000 to be spent on Bronx River restoration projects, Carter was intrigued. "Sounds like a great idea," she said, "but I don't live near the Bronx River." As previously mentioned, she lived in circumstances similar to Alexie Torres-Fleming's, and the river had always been obscured from view despite the fact that it flowed less than two blocks from Carter's childhood home. But fortuitously, she had rescued and adopted a dog she found tied to a fence post one rainy night. Emboldened to follow her down an unexplored dead-end street one day, Carter suddenly found herself at the river's edge. As she puts it, "It was beautiful in the early morning light. It was inspiring. And suddenly I

"One challenge was persuading people to join a cause when their home turf was deemed worthless by almost every action made by local, state, and federal government."

knew that this forgotten little street end, like the dog that brought me there, was worth saving."

The discovery led her to reconsider Jenny Hoffner's request for help. Carter's parents had encouraged her to do well in school, which they saw as the best way of improving her life circumstances. She excelled, and later went on to attend college and graduate school on scholarships. Then she returned to the Bronx to work for The Point Community Development Corporation, an economic development–oriented nonprofit, which was where she was when Hoffner called on her. "My interests always drew me back to the environment," she says, "from my early support of recycling."

Two issues rekindled her environmental focus: an asthma rate in the South Bronx twelve times higher than the national average, and an urban forestry report from the University of Chicago, describing how trees filter the air. In response to the forestry report, Carter spearheaded an aggressive neighborhood tree-planting campaign. The asthma epidemic stemmed largely from the area's proximity to four elevated highways, a major transfer station, and sewage treatment and sludge plants, requiring more than eleven thousand truck trips a day. And when another transfer station to handle 40 percent of New York City's trash was proposed for the Hunt's Point waterfront, she grew increasingly alarmed.

Hunt's Point is the location of the largest produce market terminal in the United States, handling approximately half of all the produce sold in the New York metropolitan area. Carter worked to defeat the proposed transfer station, convincing others they could make that happen, asking for their help, procuring seed money, and planning events and outreach to publicize the cause.

While at The Point CDC, Carter also created a public art project using "street trees" made from eclectic objects and materials and displayed for members of the community. Shortly thereafter she discovered the river, and subsequently she and The Point joined the Bronx River Working Group. As her participation in the Working Group grew, so too did her expertise and leadership capabilities.

In 2001 Carter became founding executive director of a new nonprofit organization, Sustainable South Bronx, to more fully address the issues facing the South Bronx waterfront. "One challenge was persuading people to join a cause when their home turf was deemed worthless by almost every action made by local, state, and federal government," she asserts. "The main issue was not simply that the South Bronx was ugly and dirty—rather that land use and zoning policy decisions helped to perpetuate the conditions and problems." Something

The Unintended Consequences of Success

As one raises the quality of life in a community, the phenomenon of "reverse displacement" may occur through gentrification and elevated rents. How can that result be avoided? In speaking with executive director Linda Cox, I learned that the Bronx River Alliance and its member groups are actively seeking to find more opportunities to keep community control of land along the river. According to Linda, Youth Ministries for Peace and Justice is taking the lead on identifying parcels for possible community ownership. In addition, ongoing discussion is occurring around where and what kind of landholding entities would be the most appropriate owners.

Another perplexing question is: How is increased usage along the river going to affect the wildlife so painstakingly encouraged to return? In addition to an increasing number of birds during migration season, muskrat, herons, egrets, songbirds, and raccoons have been spotted using the river. According to Brian Aucoin, the Bronx River Alliance's conservation manager, this issue forces them to walk a fine line—for example, between keeping the river open and navigable for small boats, and creating and maintaining wildlife habitat. "In years past," he says, "when a tree fell across the river forming a blockage, the entire tree would be removed for canoe and kayak access, despite the aquatic habitat forming there. We now strive to keep as much woody debris in the river as possible, while allowing on-water navigability. In-channel woody debris is beneficial for rivers, especially for such a silted and shallow river, because it increases dissolved oxygen levels and creates deeper and cooler pockets of water. This, in turn, encourages aquatic diversity, as well as giving the canoeist and kayaker a challenging run downriver."

about this scenario had to change.

Sustainable South Bronx and its Ecological Restoration Workforce Development Program soon offered programs with hands-on tasks such as training youth in riverine and estuarine restoration, including salt marsh restoration, streambed stabilization, and riparian planting projects along the Bronx River.

Bronx River Alliance Partners and Supporters

(This section suggests the breadth of constituent support that can be enlisted to help. Consideration of both likely and unlikely partners is, therefore, very important.)

Community-Based Organizations: Harding Park Homeowners Association, MBD Community Housing, Phipps Community Development Corporation, The Point Community Development Corporation, West Farms Friends of the Bronx River, Youth Ministries for Peace and Justice, Nos Quedamos, Woodlawn Taxpayers Association, Wakefield Taxpayers & Civic League, Mosholu Preservation Corporation, Hill Avenue Block Association, Neighborhood Initiatives Development Corporation, Sustainable South Bronx, Rocking the Boat, Bissel Gardens, Bronx River Art Center and Gallery

Nongovernmental Organizations: Bronx River Restoration Project, Inc., Gaia Institute, Wildlife Conservation Society/Bronx Zoo, Partnerships for Parks, Appalachian Mountain Club, Bronx River Parkway Reservation Conservancy, Neighborhood Open Space Coalition, Bronx Council for Environmental Quality, Christodora, Inc., League of Conservation Voters, Save the Sound, Transportation Alternatives, New York Restoration Project, Tri-State Transportation Campaign, New York Botanical Garden, Waterfront Park Coalition, Bronx Historical Society, Trust for Public Land, Working Waterfront Association, American Museum of Natural History, Hudson Basin River Watch

State and Local Government: City of New York/Parks & Recreation, New York State Attorney General's Office, Bronx Borough President's Office, Urban Park Rangers, City of New York Department of Transportation, Cornell Cooperative Extension/City of New York, Department of Environmental Protection, Department of Environmental Conservation, City of New York Soil & Water Conservation District, New York State Department of Transportation, Westchester County Soil & Water Conservation District, Westchester County Parks, Recreation, and Conservation, Westchester County Planning Department

Federal Government: Office of Congressman Jose Serrano, National Park Service, U.S. Department of Housing and Urban Development, U.S. Fish & Wildlife Service, U.S. Department of Agriculture/Forest Service, U.S. Department of Agriculture/NRCS, U.S. Environmental Protection Agency, National Oceanic & Atmospheric Administration, U.S. Army Corps of Engineers

Businesses: Consolidated Edison, Patagonia

Schools: Lehman College, Maritime College, South Bronx High School, Bronx Outreach High School, Fannie Lou Hamer School, MS 80, MS 45, Bronx New School, Astor Day Treatment Program, IS 20, Grace Dodge High School, Eight Plus Learning Academy, Satellite Academy (Bronx), Fordham University

Supporters: New York City Parks Foundation, Regional Plan Association, Pratt Institute/Center for Community & Environmental Development, Community Boards

Like Dart Westphal, Carter stresses the importance of seizing the moment and building on success. In fact, she briefly ran for city council after joining the Bronx River Working Group, "to help change the policies that imprison the Bronx," as she puts it. But she abandoned that pursuit for the chance to direct Sustainable South Bronx. "More doing, less talking," she says, in simple explanation.

Recently, Sustainable South Bronx received a grant for the Bronx River Greenway from the Active Living by Design Program of the Robert Wood Johnson Foundation, one of twenty-five projects chosen nationwide. This program promotes partnerships helping "to increase active living—a way of life that integrates physical activity into daily routines." Each partnership receives a $200,000 grant to address community design, land use, transportation, architecture, trails, parks, and other issues influencing healthier lifestyles. And the riverside junkyard that she discovered with her dog ended up as the recipient of the initial $10,000 grant. As Carter proudly notes, that money has been leveraged more than three hundred times. The refuse is gone and a beautiful park is under construction. Already a gathering place, it will soon become an integral part of community life in the South Bronx.

Success is empowering. "Joining that river restoration project changed my life," Carter says emphatically. "Now we have something to show for it, and something

to share—not something to prove." And, as she puts it, "You have to start some-where. Just showing up is half the battle." Majora Carter and Sustainable South Bronx are on a roll, and they are open to learning and accomplishing even more.

Planning for the Future

By 2001, with seventy-six partners involved in the restoration effort, the Bronx River Working Group needed a more defined vehicle to implement its plans and provide river stewardship. In response, the Bronx River Alliance was created in November of that year. Its mission was "to serve as a coordinated voice for the river, and work in harmonious partnership to protect, improve, and restore the Bronx River corridor and greenway so they can be healthy ecological, rec-reational, educational, and economic resources for the communities through which the river flows."

As the Alliance geared up in 2002, Jenny Hoffner stepped aside as coordina-tor after cultivating the structure and local leadership best suited to sustaining the Bronx River Project going forward. This shift occurred after an enormously productive tenure of a relatively short four and a half years in duration on Hoffner's part, and as intended from the start by the Partnerships for Parks. The board then selected Linda Cox as the first Bronx River Alliance executive direc-tor. Before departing, Hoffner inventoried her duties as coordinator, listing tasks, time frames, and the persons most likely to accomplish them. The board then prioritized the list, a move that proved most helpful to this group in transition. And, because the board had established a comprehensive succession plan looking forward four years in terms of outreach, education, and short-term, achievable projects, Cox began her new job with ample support.

A former city planner and program officer for the Lila Wallace-Readers Digest Fund, Linda Cox brought an appropriate mix of skills and perspectives to the job. At the Wallace Fund her focus had been on building community

ABOVE: Restoration projects come in all shapes and sizes; people with all levels of skills and experience gather to accomplish them. What they share is the passion and commitment to return the Bronx River to a healthy place. **RIGHT:** The National Guard moving the carcasses of several old cars from the river. They positioned a 10-ton amphibious tank wrecker called a HEMMET on an on-ramp to the Cross Bronx Expressway to lift the cars out.

participation and responsive government relations. During the 1990s the Wallace Fund sponsored many good urban park projects, and thus she saw an impressive national array of efforts. As Cox explains it, she was drawn to work for the Alliance because it clearly represents "community revitalization and establishing a visible and winning pattern." In her mind, her job at the Alliance involves working the territory between government and the community.

After serving as executive director for a year, Linda lists some of the challenges that she faces: keeping the Alliance vision compelling as it becomes increasingly institutionalized and bureaucratic—a problem common to most growing organizations; holding on to the Alliance's special role as a grassroots organization uniting a broad spectrum of people of all ages around a common purpose; avoiding losing people and energy during the transition from a working group to an alliance, when details might overwhelm or crowd out volunteers; and finding ways to encourage people to help when their interests lie in doing hands-on fieldwork, as opposed to sitting in necessarily long meetings as the project scope expands.

From early on in the Bronx River Working Group collaboration, partners have been divided into four teams focusing on four components: Education, Ecology/Restoration, the Greenway, and Outreach. Each team comprises both community and government representatives to share information and work out issues. For the Bronx River Alliance, "as with the Working Group," Linda says,

"the idea was to bring everyone to the table on the same footing. Now the Alliance creates opportunities for these teams to cross-pollinate ideas."

The Alliance's overall plan includes a number of complementary elements, including the Bronx River Greenway, an eight-mile-long trail corridor along the river, comprising a small section of the East Coast Greenway (a trail in the works, stretching the length of the East Coast from Maine to Florida—see Resources). The Bronx River Greenway will link to an existing fifteen-mile greenway upstream in Westchester County once a mile-long gap at the southern end is constructed. The full trail is due for completion in 2008, spurred on recently by the reallocation of $9 million orchestrated by U.S. Congressman Jose E. Serrano, a staunch Alliance supporter. Originally those monies were earmarked for the proposed Sheridan Expressway truck route, near the now-defunct concrete plant in the process of becoming the ten-acre Concrete Plant Park, thanks to the work of the Alliance and its partners. When members of the community helped to defeat the truck route proposal, they requested that the funds be subsequently shifted to the greenway project. Alliance members are particularly excited about moving forward because the money came even as New York City's capital budget was cut.

A second element of the Alliance plan is an Ecology and Management Program, which seeks to "promote the protection, restoration, and management of the terrestrial and aquatic resources of the Bronx River watershed through rigorous and sound planning, research, and community stewardship." Included in this program are weekly reconnaissance trips to monitor the condition of the river and to plan for its management needs. Small-scale restoration efforts such as cleanups to help maintain overall river health and habitat are undertaken using community groups as volunteer labor pools. Other large-scale efforts requiring heavy equipment or specialized expertise pair professional restoration teams with local volunteers.

A third element envisioned by Alliance members to help make the restoration more relevant to the lives of community residents is an environmental education program. Its purpose is to position the Bronx River Watershed as a critical component of school and community education curricula by promoting both the river and its watershed as a local educational resource. Guided by members of the Education Team, the program comprises teachers, scientists, and community educators actively involved in efforts along the river—a process known in

The Bronx River Alliance: Guiding Values

Value Statement: The Bronx River Alliance is committed to practicing and upholding the values of inclusion, collaboration, environmental justice, responsiveness, communication, ecological restoration, innovation, respect, integrity, and public access. These statements taken together represent the overarching values of the Bronx River Alliance. They do not stand alone; rather, each complements and supports the others in guiding us in how to achieve our vision and mission.

1] **Inclusion:** We value the full range of human diversity and seek to involve diverse populations in our staff, board, volunteers, and partners.

2] **Collaboration:** We value working together with a wide range of partners to bring together the resources, perspectives, and ideas necessary to realize our vision.

3] **Environmental Justice:** We value environmental justice and community empowerment, through commitments to public participation, principles of sustainability, transparency, and self-determination.

4] **Responsiveness:** We are committed to responding to the ever-changing needs along the river dynamically and creatively.

5] **Communication:** We have an obligation to communicate. Here we take the time to talk with one another and to listen. We believe that information is meant to move, and that information moves people.

6] **Urban Ecology/ Ecological Restoration:** We believe that connecting people both physically and emotionally to the river deepens the public's appreciation of nature and the commitment to protect it.

7] **Innovation:** We pride ourselves on executing cutting-edge solutions to complex problems.

8] **Respect:** We treat others as we would like to be treated ourselves. We do not tolerate abusive or disrespectful treatment.

9] **Integrity:** We work with communities openly, honestly, and sincerely. We act with integrity, honesty, and respect; are open, honest, and fair in all relationships; and treat each other with dignity and respect.

10] **Public Access:** We work to promote physical access to and onto the river.

11] **Communities as Our Foundation:** Many of our values are born out of our desire to empower communities. We value and respect community needs, priorities, input, participation, and independence.

12] **Environment:** We will practice what we preach through use of "green products" for our operations, an office recycling program, and utilization of local businesses whenever possible.

13] **Enjoying Our Work and Each Other:** We have fun and value a sense of humor.

educational circles as "service learning" (see Bronx River Watershed Education Program box on page 156).

Other plan elements include providing technical assistance and support to community-based efforts to organize around the Bronx River and coordinating a Bronx River Watershed monitoring program to collect and share water-quality data and address potential problems.

The Collective Power to Make a Difference

Among the positive side effects arising from recent collaborations, Linda Cox has observed a rise in jobs emerging around the river—most relating to youth, youth education, and advocacy. She calls this phenomenon a "little ecosystem of jobs." The process also has encouraged joint efforts with neighboring Westchester County, which adapted several Bronx project ideas for its own uses. Shared interests include watershed planning, linking the greenway in both locations, and water-quality monitoring.

Each of these community leaders gained invaluable insight into the process

of collaboration. They learned to differentiate between the notions of community leadership versus community participation and knowing when to step in to direct or merely guide the process—lessons learned by trial and error. Other lessons include "setting your sights high while clearly articulating your values, but also remembering to back them up to give them credibility," as Jenny Hoffner describes.

Each learned about the importance of possessing abundant energy as a leader, which partners can draw on to facilitate opportunities and deal with setbacks. The Bronx River Working Group and Alliance members now know firsthand the value of bringing everyone together in the same room (or at the same table), starting at a common place, and creating a rich forum for dialogue and collaboration. If success often comes down to the commitment of the people involved, attracting support requires combining defining goals with tangible ways of reaching them—such as the hands-on programs of Youth Ministries for Peace and Justice. Project partners gained a greater understanding of the give-and-take required to help ensure each project succeeds.

As for the collection of community leaders, they no doubt have promising futures. In Hoffner's case, she recently was promoted to direct Partnerships for Parks, which works to increase community support for and involvement in parks throughout New York City. And Westphal, Torres-Fleming, and Carter continue to excel in guiding their respective organizations. In a sense they have become civic or social entrepreneurs. Increasingly, they are invited to speak on their experiences at gatherings across the country.

Along the way, several pivotal events occurred for the Bronx River Working Group, and later, for the Alliance, as many of the people involved underwent their own dramatic shifts—from community members to community leaders. These events included reclaiming and adopting Starlight Park in 1998 (although the situation remains challenging because of contamination issues), creating a park from an abandoned cement plant, defeating the proposed trash transfer station and truck route on Edgewater Road, and, soon after, creating Hunt's Point Riverside Park. Each of these efforts tested the organizing capabilities of those involved, and ultimately the experiences transformed the community as people learned of their collective power to make a difference.

Even with projects begun decades ago but allowed to languish, a confluence of events can conspire to re-create resonance and momentum. Along the Bronx River the most meaningful results occurred when the elements of timing, leadership, economics, and fresh partnerships aligned—and the community became involved. The impact of more than seventy-five partner groups converging clearly made the difference for the Bronx River. As Linda Cox reports, the combined Working Group and Alliance efforts have leveraged more than $70 million in public and private funding for Bronx River restoration projects to date. The resulting community rebirth has begun to redefine both how the Bronx views itself and how it relates to the outside world.

As participants found their voices and their stride, the Bronx River Project offered hope and momentum to a community traditionally short on both. And as Jenny Hoffner knows instinctively, Alliance members will continue to make good progress. "All the pieces are in place," she suggests. "They own it now. It's their river."

"Art helps people explore and interpret their feelings and helps them see their environment
in new ways."—June LaCombe, environmental educator, artist, and curator of sculpture

7

HAND IN HAND

Collaborative Environmental Art and Community-Building

The relationship between landscape and art, as defined through artistic interpretation or collaborative environmental art, is an emerging and significant aspect of community collaboration. In nearly every story in this book—especially in North Carolina, Maine, New York, and Wisconsin—art played an important role in revealing the community benefits of a project, building public support and enlisting broader constituencies.

Art creates a framework using the cultural history of a particular piece of land. In art, people perceive tangible, if sometimes ephemeral, images through which they can relate their love of land and place, sparking them to act. As my friend June LaCombe suggests, "It is through the *envisioning* process that [collaborative environmental] art helps build community. Whether while contemplating the work of an individual artist, or through artists working with groups to focus on a particular issue, art helps people explore and interpret their feelings and helps them see their environment in new ways." Art can inspire greater environmental awareness, leading to advocacy and encouraging a whole new level of stewardship for the land.

Many of the communities profiled in this book use art in this way. In North Carolina, Pocosin Arts has made art integral to rural economic

LEFT: "Connor Playing to the Cows," a favorite among hundreds of community photographs collected in Richford, Vermont.

development. By creating workshop space and a gallery, it draws artists to the town of Columbia, the seat of Tyrrell County. The Pocosin Arts projects complement the environmental tourism components of the Vision 2000 plan, drawing support from further afield than would more limited offerings (see Chapter 5). As part of the Bronx River Restoration Project, art played a significant role by introducing the "Golden Ball," a National Park Service Art & Community Landscapes project. Here, to call attention to the abiding relationships between river communities, a golden sphere was transported downriver by canoe, symbolizing the sun, spirit and energy of the river. The street tree exhibits and compelling words written on found objects at the Sustainable South Bronx office and in small pocket parks near the river also gave expression to people's strong feelings about where they live (see Chapter 6 and Resources). The owners of Common Harvest Farm in Wisconsin held an art contest, encouraging farm members to express themselves through their relationship to the Earth and their love for the land—in this case, the farm (see Chapter 2). Seeking to expand their base of support, Portland Trails in Maine incorporated a variety of artistic interpretations into their promotional materials and sponsored public art in places along their trails (see Chapter 1).

Greenmuseum.org, based in Corte Madera, California, is an online, nonprofit clearinghouse formed to promote place-based art installations and the collaborative efforts necessary to create them, as well as to catalyze new opportunities. Because much of environmental art can be temporary in duration, the greenmuseum.org online showcase serves to spread the word and encourage people to take ideas back to their own communities, where they can use them in their own manner.

Examples on the site include a project by Israeli artist Shai Zakai, called Concrete Creek. For years, excess construction cement was poured into a creek near Beit Shemesh, Israel. Shai Zakai called attention to this problem through advocacy, site restoration, and public art installations and succeeded in halting the dumping altogether. Working with local quarry owners, the artist installed barrier flags in cookie cutter shapes made from collected cement and set into the stream. The cement was used to create art objects and installations, calling attention to the ongoing pollution issue and helping to raise money for cleanup efforts to remove cement debris from the creek bed.

Another project featured by greenmuseum.org, AMD&ART in Vintondale, Pennsylvania, is a collaborative effort by a group of artists, historians, and scientists. The group worked with the people of Vintondale to transform a landscape polluted by coal mining and acid mine drainage into an artful public park that

National Park Service
Rivers & Trails Program

Art
AND COMMUNITY LANDSCAPES

"PINNACLE MOUNTAIN FROM THE END OF STEVENS MILLS SLIDE ROAD" *Photo by Ashley Kittell, Richford, VT*

functions as a passive water-treatment system.

In Richford, Vermont, as part of the National Park Service Art & Community Landscapes program, residents, two sculptors, and a poet partnered with the Northern Forest Canoe Trail (see Resources), a historic, 740-mile canoe route being reestablished through four northern New England states, to interpret the meaning of community. Here the partners distributed cameras and journals to the community, inviting them to photograph and write about the people, places, traditions, objects, and activities that, to them, showed the most meaningful aspects of life in Richford. They collected more than one thousand photographs as a result, providing an eclectic, comprehensive, and sometimes surprising portrait of life in a rural New England community.

Artists and Communities Working Together

Art represents an effective way of bringing community into projects through collective envisioning, funding, siting, and maintaining the installations. It calls for artists and communities to work together. Art offers itself as cultural memory to help remind people of their place in the community. Anyone, of any age or educational background, can express through art why he or she cares about a place.

It is important to remember, however, that a fine line exists between making art and modifying or destroying natural landscapes to create it. The value and appreciation of artistic creations depends on the intention and the context in which they take place. For some, "fairy houses" (tiny dwellings built in the woods from small, natural objects found nearby) and cairns (piles of stones used as directional indicators along trails) are magical. Others perceive the disturbance of natural features for the sake of art as near blasphemy. Because of our belief in freedom of expression, we Americans sometimes do not know when to stop! Perhaps we could be more thoughtful about leaving things in their natural state in the wilderness, instead concentrating our art more in urban-oriented settings. Some feel just as strongly about not disturbing those areas, such as those who wanted to keep the Portland, Maine, rail yard along the Eastern Promenade in its raw, glass-strewn, and derelict character, rather than to create a scenic, harborfront trail for many more people to access and enjoy. One certainty is that people rarely agree on what constitutes art. And artists often seek to provoke debate and reaction through their work.

In its most positive light, however, art is transformative, teaching new ways of looking at land—the places we love—and how to protect them. As my friend and colleague Julie Isbill says, "Some art points to natural places; some prays to them." Whatever works for you, please think about how you might best use art to enhance your own causes and draw people in to support them. (More information on projects described here is available in the Resources section at the end of this book.)

EPILOGUE

Just as this book was in the finishing stages, I traveled with Virginia Farley, my friend and colleague from Vermont, to Ireland—a place dear to both our hearts. For several years we had talked about making time to meet with conservationists there about creating greater connection between our two countries. Finally, in yet another example of exquisite synchronicity, this spring we decided to seize the opportunity and go.

During the last decade, Ireland has experienced a true economic boom, largely because of the technological phenomenon known as the "Celtic Tiger." In that time, the country has gone from being among the poorest in Europe to the wealthiest. In comparison, the U.S. has had more than sixty years to deal with its surging post-World War II economy and the accompanying upheaval—both positive, as in a raised standard of living, and negative, as in unchecked land development. In contrast, Ireland has had little more than a decade to adapt. Her people are losing their heritage at a fast pace, without adequate policies and regulations in place to guide the rampant growth occurring due to this newly acquired wealth. Their challenge is daunting, and time is of the essence.

Yet even the more seasoned practitioners among us have much to learn from the Irish people—especially in their abiding relationship to the land over many centuries, despite unimaginable hardships and threats from those wishing to steal it from them. In short, the timing for further investigation seemed ripe to Virginia and me—the energy exists, as does the enthusiasm on all sides.

LEFT: The west coast of Ireland near Ballyvaughan.

While traveling from Dublin to the west coast, we spoke with a range of knowledgeable and passionate advocates—people from government agencies, funding sources, and nonprofit organizations. For us, none was more compelling than our visit with members of the Burren Action Group in County Clare, who joined forces to protect a field below the sacred mountain at Mullaghmore. Here, a proposed location of a visitor center threatened the ragged beauty of the Burren's renowned karst limestone formations—a unique ecosystem where wildflowers bloom abundantly between the craggy rocks each spring. For nine years these people summoned inordinate amounts of courage, strength, and stamina not only to challenge the government proposal, but also to oppose their neighbors and, in some instances, their own families, who saw this development as a potential economic development windfall.

The ensuing debate became acrid and emotional, ripping the community apart. The Action Group members argued that a visitor center should be sited in a village with existing services, not in a sensitive core area of the Burren National Park. When it was over, the small organization had won in court, with help from many others from across Ireland. But the price of victory was high; the wounds remain raw and their legal debt, soaring.

Despite all this, the group is in the process of healing. As time passes, they find themselves seeking to present a more positive image by focusing on ways to engage young people in carrying forward the message of protecting their heritage. At a meeting of group members at a local pub one night, Virginia and I listened, rapt, as person after person shared their poignant stories with us. We learned how the experience inspired some of their children to make a difference in their own ways, initially by studying planning, law, and environmental studies in college. We left, touched by the level of faith and tenacity they possessed, and determined to create a meaningful exchange to help them to regroup and carry on with their important mission.

The Burren Action Group story, like all those contained in this book, summons the clear affirmation that wherever I looked, I saw people responding to "the music of the wind," as farmer and group member Patrick McCormack calls it. The places and the language of the heart resonate deeply and universally. Passion inspires action, action leads to change. People everywhere feel compelled to show up—to step forward and hold fast to what they know to be priceless in their lives and for their families.

You, too, can answer this call. Just get started. People will notice and fall in beside you to help. It's amazing when that happens—and it *does* happen. Then keep your eyes on the horizon and move on ahead. This work matters so very much—to our world, and to ourselves.

BELOW: The Poulnabrone Dolmen, an ancient tomb dating back to 2500 BC, found in the Burren, County Clare, Ireland.

How to Get There from Here

STEPPING STONES

After hearing and interpreting the stories for this book, I noticed a series of common themes. They reaffirmed the far-reaching benefits of community collaboration that I had learned at Portland Trails. I think of these transcendent elements as golden threads, weaving a tapestry filled with vision and experience. At the center lie the individual strands: finding one's own—and also kindred—voices and passions; discovering hidden skills or talents; forging lasting friendships; learning to listen better and not to prejudge people and their motives; making meaningful contributions to our families and to society; thinking "big" and daring to take risks; kindling leadership potential.

The next section of the tapestry is filled with pieces local in nature: strengthening communities by building citizen participation and depth of leadership; sparking greater democracy by encouraging citizens to act; uniting former adversaries by better understanding them; and reducing societal isolation by teaching us to function in an inclusive manner. Finally, overall, a global weave completes the piece, as newly minted environmentalists and stewards step forward and encourage future generations to become ardent advocates for the Earth.

Take a look at the following questions and suggestions. Seasoned practitioners will tell you that the questions represent the most important part of the process. Questioning means you are mindful of the complexities involved and of balancing those factors as well as possible. Then you must take a leap of faith, while remembering to keep your eyes on the horizon when challenges arise. For surely they will surface!

These ideas came from many people (my advisory committee, research, and story subjects), as well as from my own experience. This is not intended to be a checklist; rather, it is a menu of helpful considerations. But be forewarned: this list may be too complex to absorb all at once. Check back from time to time, with particular topics in mind, to see if something resonates for you.

Once you have determined the most reasonable course of action, take some ideas, add more, consult with your colleagues (or find new ones to help you), and weave your own good stories.

HOW DO WE GET STARTED?

→ Use your instincts to take the first step; select the one that feels right to you.

→ Choose good projects to inspire and remind people what's worth putting time into.

→ Articulate a clear vision for your project to get people engaged in helping.

→ Brainstorm the big picture, and then focus initially on what is actually achievable.

→ Create a slogan or title that best captures your cause. Test it on people not directly involved to see how it resonates with them, not just to your "choir."

→ Shift your focus toward people and away from buildings, statistics, and results.

→ Identify the key person to direct your project, and clearly define his or her role.

→ Establish a consistent presence: a mailing address, phone, e-mail address, and office, if possible, so people know where and how to contact you.

→ Determine what makes your project unique and figure out a way to highlight or differentiate it from other causes.

→ Remember to be well prepared, and speak from your heart. You only have one chance to make a good first impression.

→ Practice more doing, less talking, as does Majora Carter of the Bronx River Alliance. Talking goes only so far. Enthusiasm results far more readily from "doing."

→ Achieve tangible results early and often (even if they are largely symbolic at times).

→ Recognize that people don't necessarily "get something back" right away; rather, they are giving service by investing their time and energy.

→ Don't think you need advanced degrees to participate; you need one only from the Graduate School of Life and Common Sense.

→ Look at other successful initiatives. Take and adapt them to your own ideas, even if the project focus is not similar to yours. Notice how success engages supporters.

→ Observe related trends occurring around you—locally, regionally, and nationally.

→ Talk to opinion leaders about your project—local, regional, and beyond, if applicable.

→ Keep them informed.

→ Create an organizational framework that works best in your community. It need not be formalized, merely consistent.

→ Recognize that some people need to express their concerns about how things are proceeding; this tactic may reflect how they process and gauge their own interest.

→ Take a step back from the trenches periodically to determine the right questions and solutions—individually and collectively.

→ Seek to make your work or project meaningful to people's daily lives.

→ *(Use these lines to list your own ideas and advice):*

→ Incorporate and feature the emotional, aesthetic, philosophical, and economic aspects of a project to capture a broader audience.

→ _____

HOW DO WE FIND THE RIGHT PARTNERS—BOTH ORGANIZATIONS AND VOLUNTEERS?

→ Take a step back to strategize; be realistic about time frame, funding, political and economic climate, and other elements affecting finding good volunteers.

→ Understand who cares about, and will be affected by, your project, as did The Nature Conservancy in forming the Rocky Mountain Front Advisory Committee.

→ Choose people (and organizations) who will work constructively and positively.

→ Work in concert with municipal, corporate, and government entities. They add value—credibility, expertise, funding, and in-kind support—as did Portland Trails, the Bronx River Alliance, the Rocky Mountain Front Advisory Committee, the Vision 2000 planners, and the Canyon Lake Creek Community Forest partners.

→ Acknowledge that outsiders need to prove themselves, but, once they do, they can bring a great deal to the mix, as shown in all six stories.

→ Involve people you think may be difficult from the start; you do not want surprises near the end. Encourage them to participate. Accommodate them as much as possible.

→ Listen for the common thread to be revealed by both likely and unlikely partners.

→ Cast a wide net to consider all possible constituents. Keep the door open for more.

→ Recognize that good volunteers are invaluable—and hard to come by. They take careful cultivation.

HOW DO WE FIND THE RESOURCES WE NEED?

→ Cast a wide net and winnow down the possibilities.

→ Get to know members, your board, constituents, and partners, so you can call on them for targeted assistance. (But be sure your mission and message is consistent.)

→ Promote the value of in-kind donations of materials and/or labor.

→ Use advisers outside your immediate circle for feedback. You might well end up enlisting them to help. But keep them informed!

→ Create a menu of options for attracting donations from individuals, corporate, municipal, state, federal agencies, and foundations.

→ Develop good relationships and communication with potential funders for future reference.

→ Be straightforward, don't embellish—it could backfire!

→ If turned down, call to ask why. Those conversations are helpful now and in the future. Remember that "no" doesn't mean "no" forever. Circumstances change.

→ Consider procuring an initial "challenge grant" to entice others to chip in too.

→ *If you don't at least ask, you'll have no chance at all!*

→ _____

HOW CAN WE GET THE WORD OUT MORE EFFECTIVELY? HOW DO WE WORK WITH THE MEDIA?

→ Communicate regularly, using compelling, professional-looking graphics and promotional materials. Look for volunteers possessing related skills to help.

→ Establish a visible pattern and winning tone to your communications.

→ Feature the works of a variety of people/volunteers in your publications and at events.

→ Determine appropriate media contacts and potential supporters in print and broadcast markets. Add them to your mailing list and inform them of newsworthy events.

→ Consider this work as political organizing—it *is* a campaign!

→ Feature a variety of artists and artistic interpretations. Recognize art as a catalyst for greater environmental awareness and action.

→ Collect and display testimonials from people with broad interests and skills enjoying your project; they speak volumes!

→ Encourage and acknowledge children as future stewards for your project, but also recognize the importance of education at all ages, as did Portland Trails.

→ Grow a comprehensive e-mail list— it's a cheap and effective way to communicate.

→ Observe and save publications you like. Borrow them to use in your own way.

→ Hold a series of fun and complementary events to feature your project, as did the Bronx River Alliance. Positive word of mouth brings people to help.

→ If you are going to create a T-shirt, make the design (and color) a smashing one!

→ _____

HOW DO WE DEFINE COMMUNITY? WHOM DO WE SERVE?

→ Community is formed through common experience and reciprocity.

→ A greater sense of community cannot be forced; it must be developed over time.

→ Your vision must be responsive to and reflective of community needs.

→ Do not underestimate the breadth of your constituents. Embrace them as they appear.

→ Brainstorm periodically with older and newer members to see if you have missed an additional constituency. Look for community in both small and large pockets.

→ Seek to accommodate differing points of view; compromise is sometimes necessary.

→ Expand your geographic area of interest if need be, as did those involved in Canyon Lake Creek Community Forest, who reached several hours away—to Seattle and beyond—for help.

→ Confer with members and the general public to ensure that your mission continues to resonate and the organization serves effectively. People will be flattered to be asked and, perhaps, further engaged in your cause.

→ _____

HOW DO WE KEEP ENTHUSIASM AND MOMENTUM GOING THROUGH THE LONG HAUL?

→ Prioritize tasks and find people with a variety of interests, skills, and strengths to accomplish them.

→ Recognize that positive people are more persuasive. Make them spokespeople.

→ Celebrate often, as does Common Harvest Farm, even when things seem bleak.

→ Understand that rhythms and opportunities wax and wane like anything else.

→ Acknowledge contributions of time and funding often. Give credit where it is due. Doing so will not dilute your organization's reputation, only enhance it.

→ Pause periodically to take stock of what is working and what needs improvement.

→ Keep your eyes on the big picture, especially during tough times.

→ Take small steps, or even backward steps, when necessary.

→ Take risks when appropriate; confer with colleagues and use your instincts to know the difference between justifiable hesitation and "nothing ventured, nothing gained."

→ Leave room for good ideas to form, and for new people possessing them.

→ Be realistic about estimating and articulating the time aspect. These projects almost *always* take a notoriously long time to implement. Long-term relationships are key.

→ Remember that how long it took doesn't matter; what matters is that it happened! When looking back, you will not recall the agony as readily as you will the triumphs.

→ Understand that the process itself is invaluable. The magic occurs during the journey.

→ Know that if the idea is good, the people, timing, and events will come together to make it possible. Yet sometimes even a good idea will languish until the time is right.

→ Remember that progress is hard to judge objectively when you are in the middle of it. You are likely doing better than you think.

→ Ask the opinion of someone outside the process to help gauge your momentum.

→ Stress that any good project is worth doing *well*.

→ Encourage your volunteers by saying, "Just showing up is half the battle." It is!

→ _____

HOW CAN WE COME TO AGREEMENT WHEN THERE ARE SO MANY DIFFERENT INTERESTS?

→ Recognize the importance of building personal relationships. They often can bridge philosophical gaps, as shown by the Rocky Mountain Front Advisory Committee.

→ Acknowledge the value of each person's contribution, regardless of size or duration.

→ Build community and political networks to create a solid foundation for your project.

→ Find the common interests among your partners. Use them as a framework.

→ Throw out the "labels" for people and focus on common values.

→ Listen to what people say and why they say it. Look for "the music behind the words." (Thank you, Alan Caron!)

→ _____

A FEW OF US DO MOST OF THE WORK—HOW DO WE BRING IN MORE PEOPLE AND HELP THEM TO PERFORM?

→ Take a step back to get an overview of the issues, people, and politics for clarity.

→ Strategize to make your message more relevant, and to attract greater support.

→ Define roles and tasks well, starting with the whole group and narrowing down.

→ Don't overlook potential constituents or interests; those working on the Canyon Lake Creek Community Forest achieved success by considering many possible groups and their viewpoints.

→ Foster public imagination around your project, and ways to capture and present it.

→ Look to newcomers seeking ways to get involved in their communities.

→ Get to know people before assigning tasks; strive to make a good fit. Mismatches waste precious time and energy.

→ Empower people to succeed. Start small if necessary and build from there.

→ Be willing to shift volunteer roles around if necessary.

→ Develop training and mentoring processes to encourage new people to join in.

→ Create effective, cohesive teams to work together on challenging or lengthy issues.

→ Check in periodically on their progress. If you cannot, assign someone dependable, with consistent communications skills.

→ _____

HOW DO WE CREATE CONTINUITY AND DEPTH OF LEADERSHIP?

→ Tell people the stories behind how the idea was hatched, along with any other early history, to help them feel engaged and in the know.

→ Empower people to succeed by making their tasks distinct and achievable.

→ Allow people to help while their time, energy, and enthusiasm exists.

→ Empower people to step away with heads held high regardless of duration of service. Acknowledge them warmly when they depart or reduce their involvement.

→ Consider asking key people to stay on in an advisory capacity, as did Portland Trails.

→ Use volunteers thoughtfully and sparingly to avoid burnout or overkill.

→ Create a mentoring system, pairing seasoned with newer participants.

→ Bring people along; make them feel important and appreciated all along the way.

→ If entire families are involved, feature them; others may follow suit.

→ _____

HOW DO WE FIND AND TRAIN NEW PEOPLE BEFORE THE FOUNDERS SLIP AWAY?

→ Good projects are like magnets; they collect leaders and volunteers.

→ Cultivate a receptive attitude from the top down.

→ Set an early precedent for your volunteers largely as "doers" and less as figureheads.

→ Seek multidisciplined talent to fill in the gaps.

→ Encourage mentoring at all levels, for large or small tasks.

→ Highlight the contributions of people in all communications, giving the impression of a vibrant project and attracting others to help.

→ _____

HOW DO WE KEEP THE MOMENTUM GOING AFTER THE FOUNDERS SLIP AWAY?

→ Create a solid framework for future boards and volunteers.

→ Allow the mission and focus to evolve with the group.

→ Engage those remaining in strategic planning for the future.

→ Share the organizational stories with new people so they have a sense of context.

→ Acknowledge the roles of founders to inspire descendants and encourage continuity.

→ Encourage founders to participate in occasional events to inspire others.

→ Consider creating an advisory board to engage and retain founders in a targeted capacity, but be thoughtful about using them sparingly.

→ _____

HOW DO WE KEEP VOLUNTEERS ENGAGED AND WORKING WITH US?

→ Plant the seeds today and yield the harvest tomorrow.

→ Remember that one distinct success inspires another. Work hard to achieve them, large or small.

→ Don't promise what you can't deliver. Be realistic.

→ Instill responsibility for the future by promoting good stewardship.

→ Give volunteers real responsibility and then empower them to succeed.

→ Provide support without micromanaging.

→ Create a menu of tasks, both long- and short-term, to engage people.

→ Help them to understand how all the pieces fit together, their role included.

→ Listen to their ideas and act on the good ones, while finding a way to acknowledge all ideas.

→ _____

HOW DO WE KEEP ATTENDANCE AT MEETINGS HIGH?

→ Keep meetings relevant and on time.

→ Recognize when tangential discussion occurs; allow it when appropriate, delegate the rest to smaller groups at other times.

→ Get to know volunteers and their interests.

→ Poll participants outside of meetings when necessary to contain unanticipated responses that may derail progress.

→ Be clear about desired outcomes, roles, courteous behavior, and mutual respect for time and effort, in every meeting.

→ Determine the best time of day to hold meetings. Change occasionally if necessary.

→ Consider using revolving meeting sites to accommodate those coming from a distance.

→ Hold gatherings, potlucks, and other fun events periodically to celebrate milestones, large and small.

→ _____

HOW DO WE GET OVER OUR FEAR OF "NAYSAYERS" OR WORKING WITH CHALLENGING PEOPLE?

→ Listen to and incorporate the concerns of your potential opponents.

→ Focus on "interests" vs. "positions."

→ Recognize that self-interest may start things rolling but people can and do move beyond that point.

→ Work to accommodate new people who bring their own realities and expectations.

→ Invite challenging partners to the table, no matter how scary; just do it anyway! You will head off unexpected twists and delays late in the process.

→ Get to know people better to demystify their perspectives and opinions.

→ Make room in your hearts to listen and accept others for their own ways of caring.

→ Understand that disagreeing does not mean you can't move forward together.

→ Establish ground rules for listening, courtesy, and respect, as did the Bronx River Alliance.

→ Realize that you may be partners on one issue and foes over another. This happens all the time. Try to understand where the other person is coming from and why.

→ Speak from your heart. People will recognize that and respect you for doing so.

→ Get a mutual friend to bring "naysayers" to the table, as in the Rocky Mountain Front example.

→ _____

HOW DO WE LEARN TO COLLABORATE?

→ Learn to incorporate the strengths of all partners to make it work.

→ Learn by doing. Learn from mistakes and missed opportunities.

→ Learn to take risks. Lead by example.

→ Learn to navigate through the politics of your community.

→ Understand the normal learning curve: everyone learns from the process.

→ Focus on being present for the process of collaboration. It's a journey.

→ Bring everyone to the table on the same footing.

→ Respect individual points of view, even though you might not agree.

→ Work collaboratively through a crisis to ultimately improve projects.

→ Respond flexibly. Find ways to agree. Give and take.

→ Ask for help from those more experienced. Don't wait until you are desperate!

→ _____

HOW DO WE INCLUDE CULTURAL DIFFERENCES AND CONCERNS?

→ Invite, interpret, and share the stories of people, land, history, and culture.

→ Brainstorm and plan positive and inclusive events.

→ Ask different cultural groups to plan specific (or parts of) events.

→ Introduce differing cultural practices to give people perspective and context.

→ Understand that "one size fits-all" does not work in rural vs. urban settings.

→ Honor and facilitate the connection between different constituencies and disciplines.

→ Acknowledge and celebrate the roles played by all interests.

→ _____

HOW DO WE LEARN TO DEAL WITH THE COMPLEXITIES OF COLLABORATIVE WORK?

Sometimes good projects can have negative consequences or surprising adversaries. (For example, preserving or rehabilitating a place may force longtime residents out because of the resulting elevated land values, concerns faced by Bronx River Alliance members.)

→ Learn to recognize and acknowledge the paradox in many well-intentioned projects. The issues, options, and their consequences often are not simply black and white.

→ Consider the "ripple-effect" factor. Be willing to accommodate unforeseen results.

→ Keep your eyes always on the big picture as well as on the details.

→ Discuss and define the concepts, issues, and complexities of your project.

→ Strive to maintain traditions while accommodating healthy growth and change.

→ Recognize and explain that the "how to" and the "why" of projects are interwoven—one aspect does not, and should not, exist without the other.

→ _____

→ Recognize that successful organizations must offer multiple ways of reaching different constituencies (i.e., projects in several neighborhoods, a diverse board, and newsletter articles appealing to people with a variety of interests and backgrounds).

→ Seek connecting threads among diverse entities. Highlight and celebrate them.

→ Acknowledge that the quality of everyday life matters, as the Eastern 4-H Center does in the Tyrrell County, North Carolina, story.

→ Focus on core values in your mission. Others will recognize those you share.

→ Make your message relevant to children through education programs, outings, and visits to schools and other groups. They are your future, and they often can convince their parents to shift their habits and outlooks, as shown by Portland Trails, the Bronx River Alliance, and the Partnership for the Sounds in Tyrrell County.

→ Don't overlook engaging people of all ages. It is never too late to learn or change.

→ Realize that land conservation is a means, not an end, to creating healthy and stable communities. Make your language and actions reflect that concept.

→ _____

HOW DO WE MAKE OUR WORK RELEVANT TO PEOPLE "BEYOND THE CHOIR"?

→ Connect your project to their hearts, their families, and their common experience.

→ Promote the interconnection of loss and opportunity in jumpstarting a project.

→ Establish the importance of environmental values along with social, economic, etc.

→ Strive to embody credibility.

→ Show, don't tell. Good project results sell themselves. Gimmicks are not needed.

HOW DO WE KEEP FROM BURNING OURSELVES OUT?

→ Stay conscious of your workload and take time to get away—whether for an afternoon, a weekend, or a real vacation. You won't be any good to anyone, most of all yourself, if you don't. Just do it—don't argue! People will respect you more for taking care of yourself and your sanity.

→ Learn how to ask for help when you need it. (This is a big one.)

→ If you feel close to meltdown, share this with your most trusted colleagues. Speaking about it out loud can help to defuse the tension. Ask for their advice. Then make your own decision about what you need to do.

→ Learn how to say No! People appreciate knowing where they stand, what's possible, and what's not. Timing may be better for you later, or perhaps never. That's okay too. You can only do your best.

→ Make time to visit the places you are working so hard to save or create. Then visit them again. It's easy to lose track of the reasons behind your focus when you are mired in a million details. Being on site will ground you and reconnect you to your mission.

→ Take the time to reflect and remember why you initially took on this project. Often we become so immersed in logistics and details that we lose sight of the compelling reasons we began in the first place.

→ _____

WHAT ARE THE BENEFITS OF COLLABORATIVE, COMMUNITY-BASED WORK?

It can:

→ bring positive, tangible news in an uncertain and desperate world, as expressed by a member of Common Harvest Farm;

→ offset the tenor of the times, feelings of helplessness; this is something *you* can do;

→ facilitate significant changes in attitude from the bottom up—from the grassroots;

→ engage people who otherwise might not participate in civic service, often first-timers;

→ fuel other community-based efforts in response to impending change;

→ create reciprocity: everyone benefits, in ways they cannot begin to imagine;

→ reveal latent community leaders and activists during the course of participation;

→ build democracy in its truest form through direct participation; people often go on to other, greater efforts social, political, environmental—or a mix of elements;

→ raise environmental and health consciousness; since the 1970s, no outlets or vehicles had existed for urban or suburban dwellers until these collaborative projects surfaced;

→ give participants and beneficiaries a sense of intimacy with the natural world and natural cycles, in both urban and rural areas;

→ transport people by transforming them through broad and deep firsthand experiences;

→ introduce new ways of working and communicating—a common denominator and common language, as did the Rocky Mountain Front Advisory Committee;

→ embody positive social change and ways of being in society, as did the Bronx River Alliance mission and the Tyrrell County's Vision 2000 plan;

→ foster civic and social entrepreneurs, and environmental advocates;

→ integrate key quality-of-life elements: transportation, environment, economic development, recreation, health, and spiritual well-being, as did Portland Trails;

→ achieve success against long odds, resulting in raising the bar for other initiatives;

→ reinvigorate a collective process that worked well historically in challenging times, during war, and the Depression era;

→ give people real-life examples of successful community building;

- serve as incubators for other efforts and extend the depth of community leadership;

- create new models for working in the community, protecting the environment, and integrating economic development, as did the Tyrrell County Vision 2000 plan;

- complement government, and corporate undertakings where everyone looks good, as did the Canyon Lake Creek Community Forest project;

- make it safer for larger entities, both governmental and corporate, to take risks because of broad-based support, as did the Canyon Lake Creek project; and

- act as a sounding board for a variety of public and private issues, as did the Rocky Mountain Front Advisory Committee;

- heal the increasing division of spirituality from the Earth created by advancing science and technology, by shifting toward spirituality embodied in the natural world;

- nurture us through the "sacred" work of creating better places to live and work;

- add to self-awareness through discovering common values and caring;

- allow people to become vested in their communities in deep, meaningful ways;

- open the possibility of a shared future from an increasingly isolated society; and

- teach that individual actions do make a difference.

- ___

HOW DO WE KNOW WHEN IT IS TIME TO MOVE ON TO SOMETHING NEW?

This is important!

- Move on when you are on a roll—clearly on a high note.

- Leave before you lose enthusiasm for the project.

- Let partners and colleagues know the value that working together has brought you.

- Remember that new blood and energy are always good for keeping a project vital and effective, and for taking it to the next level.

- Know that a certain grace is necessary to know when the time is right. Pay attention!

- If appropriate, celebrate your collective journey with a festive event. Everyone involved benefits and the way opens for the next era to begin on a positive note.

- ___

RESOURCES

This section provides information about organizations referred to and related publications from each story, plus suggested additional reading. Please note that some organizations can assist you directly (❧). For more information about how they can best help, see their Web site or call them directly. Other organizations (⊹) should be used as models, to borrow from and shape to fit your own ideas.

BRONX RIVER RESTORATION PROJECT

❧ Appalachian Mountain Club
 5 Joy Street, Boston, MA 02108
 (617) 523-0655
 www.outdoors.org

❧ Bronx River Alliance
 One Bronx River Parkway, Bronx, NY 10462
 (718) 430-4665
 www.bronxriver.org

⊹ East Coast Greenway Alliance
 135 Main St., Wakefield, RI 02879
 (401) 789-4625
 www.greenway.org

✢ Institute for Local Self-Reliance
2425 18th Street NW, Washington, DC 20009
(202) 232-4108;
1313 Fifth Street SE, Minneapolis, MN 55414
(612) 379-3815
www.ilsr.org

❧ Mosholu Preservation Corporation
3400 Reservoir Oval East, Bronx, NY 10467
(718) 324-4998
www.bronxmall.com/norwoodnews

❧ National Park Service Rivers & Trails Program
15 State Street, Boston, MA 02109-3572
(617) 223-5051
www.nps.gov/rtca

❧ Partnerships for Parks, Arsenal North
1234 Fifth Ave., Rm. 234, New York, NY 10029
(212) 360-3326
www.nycgovparks.org

❧ Sustainable South Bronx
889 Hunts Point Avenue, Bronx, NY 10474
(718) 617-4668
www.ssbx.org

❧ Youth Ministries for Peace and Justice
1384 Stratford Ave., Bronx, NY 10472
(718) 328-5622

RELATED PUBLICATIONS

Partnerships for Parks, 1999, Chris Walker, The Urban Institute, available from www.uipress.org or downloadable as a pdf file from the Wallace Foundation at www.wallacefoundation.org.

The Public Value of Urban Parks, 2004, Chris Walker, The Urban Institute, available from www.uipress.org or downloadable as a pdf file from the Wallace Foundation at www.wallacefoundation.org.

Two good sites on urban parks and partnership efforts are found at the American Planning Association's City Parks Forum at www.planning.org/cpf and the Project for Public Space's site at www.urbanparks.org.

Virtual tour of the Bronx River on the NYC Parks Department's Web site: www.nycgovparks.org/sub_your_park/flagship_and_virtual.html

CANYON LAKE CREEK COMMUNITY FOREST

❧ The Trust for Public Land
Northwest Regional Office
Waterfront Place Bldg., Suite 605
1011 Western Ave., Seattle, WA 98104
(206) 587-2447
www.tpl.org

❧ The Trust for Public Land, National Office
116 New Montgomery St., Fourth Floor
San Francisco, CA 94105
(415) 495-4014
www.tpl.org

✢ Whatcom County Parks and
Recreation Department, 3373 Mount Baker
Highway Bellingham, WA 98226
(360) 733-2900
www.co.whatcom.wa.us/parks/index.jsp

✢ Whatcom Land Trust
P.O. Box 6131, Bellingham, WA 98227
(360) 650-9470
www.whatcomlandtrust.org

RELATED PUBLICATIONS

Whatcom Places: A Celebration in Words and Photographs, 1997, edited and published by the Whatcom Land Trust.

COMMON HARVEST FARM

✝ Holden Village
HC00 Stop 2, Chelan, WA 98816-9769
(No phone; external, stand alone Web site)
www.holdenvillage.org

❧ Robyn Van En Center for CSA Resources
Wilson College
1015 Philadelphia Ave., Chambersburg, PA 17201
(717) 264-4141
www.csacenter.org

✣ Standing Cedars Community Land Conservancy
P.O. Box 249, Osceola, WI 54020-0249
(715) 294-4690
www.privatelandownernetwork.org/
resource.asp?id=1004

✣ The Land Stewardship Project
2200 4th Street, White Bear Lake, MN 55110
(651) 653-0618
www.landstewardshipproject.org

✣ West Wisconsin Land Trust
500 East Main St., Suite 307, Menomonie, WI 54751
(715) 235-8850
www.wwlt.org

❧ The New Farm Web site www.newfarm.org

RELATED PUBLICATIONS

Breaking Bread: The Spiritual Significance of Food, 1992, Sara Covin Juengst, Westminster/John Knox Press.

Coming Home to Eat, 2001, Gary Paul Nabhan, W.W. Norton & Company.

Farming with the Wild: Enhancing Biodiversity on Farms and Ranches, Dan Imhoff, the Wild Farm Alliance, P.O. Box 2570, Watsonville, CA 95077 (831) 761-8408 www.wildfarmalliance.org.

Fast Food Nation: The Dark Side of the All-American Meal, 2002, Eric Schlosser, HarperCollins.

From Asparagus to Zucchini: A Guide to Farm-Fresh Seasonal Produce, the Madison Area Community Supported Agriculture Coalition (MACSAC). P.O. Box 7814, Madson, WI 53707-7814 (608) 226-0300 www.macsac.org

Hope's Edge: The Next Diet for a Small Planet, 2002, Frances Moore Lappe and Anna Lappe, Tarcher/Putnam.

Sharing the Harvest: A Guide to Community-Supported Agriculture, 1999, Elizabeth Henderson and Robyn Van En, Chelsea Green.

The Eco-Foods Guide: What's Good for the Earth is Good for You, 2002, Cynthia Barstow, New Society Publishers.

The Unsettling of America: Culture & Agriculture, 1977, Wendell Berry, Sierra Club Books.

What Are People For? 1990, Wendell Berry, Farrar, Straus and Giroux.

PORTLAND TRAILS

❧ CO-SEED, The Center for Environmental Education of Antioch New England Institute
40 Avon Street, Keene, NH 03431-3516
(603) 357-3122 x240
www.anei.org
e-mail: coseed@anei.org

❧ Maine Audubon Society, 20 Gilsland Farm Road
Falmouth, ME 04105
(207) 781-2330
www.maineaudubon.org

❧ Maine Coast Heritage Trust
1 Main Street, Suite 201, Topsham, ME 04086
(207) 729-7366
www.mcht.org

❧ Maine Land Trust Network
1 Main Street, Suite 201, Topsham, ME 04086
(207) 729-7366
www.mltn.org

❧ National Park Service Rivers & Trails
14 Maine Street, Suite 302, Brunswick, ME 04011
(207) 725-4934
www.nps.gov/rtca

✣ Portland Trails
305 Commercial Street, Portland, ME 04101
(207) 775-2411
www.trails.org

❧ The Center for Environmental Education of Antioch New England Institute
40 Avon Street, Keene, NH 03431-3516
(603) 355-3251
www.schoolsgogreen.org

✣ The Chewonki Foundation
485 Chewonki Neck Rd., Wiscasset, ME 04578-4822
(207) 882-7323
www.chewonki.org

❧ The Mountain Division Alliance
P.O. Box 532, Fryeburg, ME 04037

❧ The Orton Family Foundation
128 Merchants Row, 2nd Floor, Rutland, VT 05701
(802) 773-6336
www.orton.org

❧ The Rails-to-Trails Conservancy
1100 17th St. NW, Washington, DC 20036
(202) 331-9696
www.railtrails.org

❧ The Student Conservation Association (SCA)
689 River Road, P.O. Box 550, Charlestown, NH
03503-0550
(603) 543-1700
www.thesca.org

❧ The Trust for Public Land (Maine Field Office)
377 Fore Street, 3rd Floor, Portland, ME 04101
(207) 772-7424
www.tpl.org

THE ROCKY MOUNTAIN FRONT ADVISORY COMMITTEE

✣ Devil's Kitchen
http://water.montana.edu/watersheds/oldgroups/
details.asp?id=43

✣ The Malpai Borderlands Project
www.epa.gov/ecocommunity;/case6/malpai.htm

❧ The Nature Conservancy
4245 N. Fairfax Drive, Suite 100,
Arlington, VA 22203-1606
(800) 628-6860
www.nature.org

❧ The Nature Conservancy/Montana Chapter
32 South Ewing, Helena, MT 59601
(406) 443-0303
www.nature.org

❧ The Sonoran Institute, Main Office
7650 E. Broadway, Suite 203, Tucson, AZ 85710
(520) 290-0828
www.sonoran.org

✣ Upper and Lower San Pedro River Projects
www.nature.org (Search for specifics on each section.)

✣ Yampa Valley Partners
745 Russell Street, Craig, CO 81625
(970) 824-8233
www.yampavalleypartners.com

RELATED PUBLICATION

Beyond the Rangeland Conflict: Toward a West That Works, 1995, Dan Daggett, Gibbs Smith Press.

VISION 2000: THE TYRRELL COUNTY ECONOMIC DEVELOPMENT INITIATIVE

✣ Green Infrastructure Web site is hosted by The Conservation Fund in partnership with USDA Forest Services. Please send messages to
email@greeninfrastructure.net
www.greeninfrastructure.net

✣ Partnership for the Sounds
P.O. Box 55, Columbia, NC 27925
(252) 796-1000
www.partnershipforthesounds.org

✣ Pocosin Arts
P.O. Box 690, Columbia, NC 27925
(252) 796-2787
www.pocosinarts.org

❧ Resourceful Communities Program
visit www.resourcefulcommunities.org

❧ Rural Heritage Forum c/o Conservation Fund
P.O. Box 271, Chapel Hill, NC 27514
(919) 967-2223

✤ The Conservation Fund
1800 North Kent Street, Suite 1120, Arlington, VA 22209-2156
(703) 525-6300
www.conservationfund.org

✤ The Conservation Fund (North Carolina Office)
P.O. Box 271, Chapel Hill, NC 27514
(919) 967-2223
www.conservationfund.org

✣ The Eastern 4-H Environmental Education Conference Center
100 N. Clover Way, Columbia, NC 27925
(252) 797-4800
www.eastern4hcenter.com

✣ Tyrrell County Community Development Corporation
604 Main St., P.O. Box 58, Columbia, NC 27925
(252) 796-1991
e-mail: tccdc@mail.com

✣ Tyrrell County Visitor Center
203 South Ludington Dr., Columbia, NC 27925
(252) 796-0723

RELATED PUBLICATION

Saving America's Countryside: A Guide to Rural Conservation, 1989, 1997, Samuel N. Stokes, A. Elizabeth Watson, Shelley S. Mastran, the Johns Hopkins University Press.

REFLECTIONS ON COLLABORATIVE ENVIRONMENTAL ART AND COMMUNITY-BUILDING

✣ AMD&ART, Inc., c/o The Bottleworks
411 Third Avenue, Johnstown, PA 15906
(814) 539-5357
www.amdandart.org

✣ greenmuseum.org
518 Tamalpais Dr., Corte Madera, CA 94925
(415) 945-9322
www.greenmuseum.org

✤ National Park Service Rivers & Trails: Art and Community Landscapes Program
15 State Street, Boston, MA 02109-3572
(617) 223.5210
www.nps.gov/rtca or www.nefa.org/grantprog/acl/index.html

✣ Panorama: The North American Landscape in Art
www.virtualmuseum.ca/Exhibitions/Landscapes/index.html

✣ The Northern Forest Canoe Trail
P.O. Box 565, Waitsfield, VT 05673
(802) 496-2285
www.northernforestcanoetrail.org

RELATED PUBLICATIONS

But Is It Art? The Spirit of Art as Activism, 1995, edited by Nina Felshin, Bay Press.

Earthworks and Beyond: Contemporary Art in the Landscape, 1984, 1989, 1998, John Beardsley, Cross River Press.

Ecovention: Current Art to Transform Ecologies, 2002, Sue Spaid, The Contemporary Arts Center.

Fragile Ecologies: Contemporary Artists' Interpretations and Solutions, 1992, Barbara C. Matilsky, Rizzoli, in association with The Queens Museum of Art (out of print).

Land and Environmental Art, 1998, Jeffrey Kastner and Brian Wallis, Phaidon Press Limited.

Mapping the Terrain: New Genre Public Art, 1995, edited by Suzanne Lacy, Bay Press.

Sculpting with the Environment: A Natural Dialogue, 1995, edited by Baile Oaks (with essays from Capra, Gablic, and Berry), Van Nostrand Reinhold.

The Reenchantment of Art, 1991, Suzi Gablik, Thames and Hudson.

ArtsEdNet; www.getty.edu/education

Green Arts Web: Resource for environmental artists, offers an extensive bibliography. www.greenarts.org

EPILOGUE

✤ GroundWork
1825 Eye Street, NW, Suite 400
Washington, DC 20006
(202) 429-2070
www.groundworkers.org

✛ The Burren Action Group, County Clare, Ireland
www.iol.ie/~burrenag/

ADDITIONAL PUBLICATIONS ON RELATED TOPICS

Balancing Nature and Commerce in Gateway Communities, 1997, Jim Howe, Ed McMahon, and Luther Propst, Island Press.

Better Together: Restoring the American Community, 2003, Robert D. Putnam and Lewis M. Feldstein, with Don Cohen, Simon & Schuster.

Bowling Alone: The Collapse and Revival of American Community, 2000, Robert D. Putnam, Simon & Schuster.

Civic Environmentalism, 1994, DeWitt John, Congressional Quarterly, Inc.

Collaborative Leadership: How Citizens and Civic Leaders Can Make a Difference, 1994, David D. Chrislip and Carl E. Larson, Jossey-Bass Publishers.

Community and the Politics of Place, 1990, Daniel Kemmis, University of Oklahoma Press.

The Ecology of Hope: Communities Collaborate for Sustainability, 1997, Ted Bernard and Jora Young, New Society.

The Experience of Place, 1991, Tony Hiss, Random House, Inc.

Educating the Reflective Practitioner, 1990, Donald A. Schon, John Wiley and Sons.

Getting Started: How to Succeed in Heritage Tourism 1993, The National Trust for Historic Preservation.

Getting Together: Building Relationships as We Negotiate, 1989, Roger Fisher, Scott Brown, Penguin USA.

Getting to Yes: Negotiating Agreement Without Giving In, 1991, Roger Fisher, William Ury, and Bruce Patton, Penguin USA.

The Great Remembering, 2001, Peter Forbes, The Trust for Public Land.

Greenways for America, 1990, Charles E. Little, Johns Hopkins University Press.

Heart of the Land, 1994, edited by Joseph Barbato and Lisa Weinerman of The Nature Conservancy, Random House, Inc.

Hope for the Land, 1992, Charles E. Little, Rutgers University Press.

The Landscape of Conservation Stewardship (Report of the Stewardship Initiative Feasibility Study), 2000, Jacquelyn L. Tuxill.

The Lure of the Local: Senses of Place in a Multicultural Society, 1997, Lucy Lippard, The New Press.

Making Collaboration Work: Lessons from Innovation in Natural Resource Management, 2000, Julia M. Wondolleck and Steven L. Yaffee, Island Press.

The New Agrarianism: Land, Culture, and the Community of Life, 2001, edited by Eric T. Freyfogle, Island Press.

NPS Rivers and Trails Community Tool Box, 2001, National Park Service Rivers & Trails Program. Available for free download at www.nps.gov.rtca.

Organizing Outdoor Volunteers, 1992, Roger L. Moore, Vicki LaFarge, Charles L. Tracy, Appalachian Mountain Club Books. (Difficult to find.)

O, Say, Can You See: A Visual Awareness Toolkit for Communities, 1999, M. Maguire, C. Truppi, R Hawks, J. Palmer, C. Doble, S. Shannon, S. Stokes, and S. Morris, the National Park Service.

Our Land, Ourselves, 1999, edited by Peter Forbes, Ann Armbrecht Forbes, Helen Whybrow, The Trust for Public Land.

Partnerships in Communities: Reweaving the Fabric of Rural America, 2000, Jean Richardson, Island Press.

Reconstructing Conservation: Finding Common Ground, 2003, edited by Ben A. Minteer and Robert E. Manning, Island Press.

Saving America's Countryside, 1989, 1997, Samuel N. Stokes, A. Elizabeth Watson, Shelley S. Mastran, the Johns Hopkins University Press.

Smart Growth, Better Neighborhoods: Communities Leading the Way, 2000, National Neighborhood Coalition, www.neighborhoodcoalition.com.

The Story Handbook, Conservationists 2003, edited by Helen Whybrow, The Trust for Public Land.

Sustaining Innovation: Creating Nonprofit and Government Organizations that Innovate Naturally, 1998, Paul C. Light, John Wiley & Sons, Inc.

Turning to Earth: Stories of Ecological Conversion, 2003, F. Marina Schauffler, University of Virginia Press.

OTHER GOOD RESOURCES

The Center for Whole Communities
Knoll Farm, 700 Bragg Hill Rd., Fayston, VT 05673
(802) 496-5690
www.wholecommunities.org. This nonprofit runs a unique leadership forum called the Refuge for Land and People, where citizens and activists from around the country come together to find solutions to the most pressing and difficult conservation issues our nation faces today. The Refuge is the campfire around which diverse sectors of the land community—urban and rural land trusts, wilderness and farmland advocates, ranchers, biologists, writers and educators, environmental justice advocates—engage with one another to nurture a shared vision for how conservation can become a more powerful force for cultural change.

The Conservation Study Institute
54 Elm St., P.O. Box 178, Woodstock, VT 05091
(802) 457-3368
www.nps.gov/mabi/csi, established by the National Park Service, contributes to leadership in the field of conservation. The Institute creates opportunities for dialogue, inquiry, and lifelong learning to enhance the stewardship of landscapes and communities.

Energize, Inc. is an international training, consulting, and publishing firm specializing in volunteerism. Founded in 1977, Energize has assisted organizations of all types with their volunteer efforts. Their Web site offers a comprehensive library of publications for sale: www.energizeinc.com.

The Northern Forest Center
P.O. Box 210, Concord, NH 03302-0210
(603) 229-0679
www.northernforest.org is a nonprofit organization formed "to mobilize people to build healthy communities, economies, and ecosystems by working together across the Northern Forest region" of New England.

QLF/Atlantic Center for the Environment
55 South Main Street, Ipswich, MA 01938
(978) 356-0038
www.qlf.org is a nonprofit organization whose mission is to support the quality of life and environment for persons living in rural areas of eastern Canada and New England. QLF programs that promote natural resource conservation and leadership training—through environmental education, wildlife research, land stewardship, and international exchanges—are conducted by QLF's Atlantic Center for the Environment.

Rails to Trails Conservancy
1100 17th Street, NW, 10th Floor
Washington, DC 20036
(866) 202-9788
www.railtrails.org is dedicated to enriching America's communities and countryside by creating a nationwide network of public trails from former rail lines and connecting corridors.

The Land Trust Alliance
1331 H St., NW, Suite 400
Washington, DC 20005-4734
(202) 638-4725
www.lta.org serves as the umbrella organization for local and regional land trusts, providing information, training, and resources that help them to conserve land.

Vital Communities
104 Railroad Row, White River Junction, VT 05001
(802) 291-9100
www.vitalcommunities.org is a nonprofit organization that works to engage citizens in community life and to foster the long-term balance of cultural, economic, environmental, and social well-being in their region. They could serve as a model for your own region.

ACKNOWLEDGMENTS

Before starting this project, I worried about the prospect of working from the corner room of my farmhouse. The potential isolation would be in direct contrast to the highly collaborative way in which I most often thrive, treasuring the constant meeting and encouraging of people to join the cause, whatever it may be.

Fortunately, my concern was short-lived. Since compiling this list of people to acknowledge, I've realized, quite obviously, what a collective effort this book has been. Without the support of so many friends, colleagues, family, and those I met through each story, this project simply would not have been possible. To all of you, and to the many others with whom I did not have the chance to talk at length, thank you for your gift of this unparalleled, inspiring, and enriching experience.

To those visionaries helping to get me started: Richard Barringer, Marcy Lyman, Elizabeth Kline, Peter Stein, and Elizabeth Watson.

Special thanks for his early, warm, and incalculable support to Peter Forbes from TPL's Center for Land and People and the Center for Whole Communities, a pioneer in the important national dialogue on creating a shared vision for how land conservation can become a more powerful force for cultural change.

LEFT: Just moments before, a 90-foot crane swung the Fore River Bridge into place in Portland, Maine.

To my chief sponsor, the Trust for Public Land and the Center for Land and People, especially Ernest Cook, Constance deBrun, Kathy Blaha, Rose Harvey, Jonathan Hopps, Amy Mullin, and Debra Summers.

To my co-sponsors, who brought me much credibility and great advice: National Park Service Rivers & Trails: Chris Brown, Sam Stokes, Steve Golden, and Steve Morris. From The Conservation Fund: Ed McMahon, Christine Fanning, and Eric Meyers. And from The Nature Conservancy: Valerie Dorian.

To my patient and thoughtful advisory board (chosen because they would tell me what they *really* thought): Burnham Martin, Chair; Rupert Neily, Laura Newman, Steve Spencer, Anne Truslow, and Lois Winter; with special editing assistance and moral support from John Monroe. Our discussions were sometimes challenging, but always enlightening.

To my friends and colleagues who lent their support and expertise: John Andrews, Jane Arbuckle, Liza Bakewell, Margo Baldwin, Steve Blackmer, Sam Bower, Heather Boyer, Elena Brandt, Sandy Buck, Deb Burd, Elizabeth Byers, Judy Carl-Hendrick, Alan Caron, Murray Carpenter, Meg Castagna, Will Childs, Michael Clarke, Jacki Cohen, Susan Connolly, Carl Demrow, everyone at Terrence J. DeWan & Associates, Stephen Dignazio, Julie Early, Jay Espy, Stephanie Gilbert, Bill Ginn, Eliza Ginn, Gordon Glover, Kate Hanson, Evan Haynes, David Heald, Tom Howe, Phil Huffman, Julie Isbill, June LaCombe, DeWitt John, Meredith Jones, Jack Kartez, Sandra Klimt, Rich Knox, Jonathan Labaree, Nancy Light, Alan Lishness, David MacDonald, Miranda Marland, Sarah Marshall, Ken Matthews, Laura McDill, Barney McHenry, John Melrose, Sam Merrill, Roger Milliken, Nora Mitchell, Bob Moore, Bo Norris, Jeff Norris, Lynne O'Hara, John Oliver, Molly Paul, Joe Payne, Gioia Perugini, Frankie Plymale, Marcel Polak, Caroline MacDonald Pryor, Keith Ross, Jenny Russell, Naomi Schalit, Marina Schauffler, Hans Schoepflin, Lynne Seeley, Sally Sheridan, Megan Shore, Moira Simonds, Alan Stearns, Lorna Stevens, Stephanie Takes-Desbiens, Ann Tartre, Charlie Tracy, Davis Thomas, Tupper Thomas, Jackie Tuxill, Tammara Van Ryn, Lissa Widdoff, Carolyn Wollen, Kent Wommack, and Marty Zeller.

To the foundations believing in the possibilities for this book to help spark emerging community activists into action, I am most grateful for your vote of confidence: the Lennox Foundation and the Panta Rhea Foundation.

To Senator George Mitchell, for lending his experience and international reputation to my foreword, and for supporting Portland Trails since its early years.

For their ongoing friendship and support of this journey in so many ways: Walter and Margaret Brewster, Marnie Brewster Phillips, Wickes Brewster, Nancy Custer Carroll, Virginia Farley, Gordon Hall, Donna Hopkins, Foster and Patti Hopkins, Suzanne Hopkins, Lucy Hull, Ron Huntley, Mary Pope Hutson, Steve and Caroline Hyde, David and Sarah Hyde, Candace Hyde and Jim Tukey, Karen Jensen, Mark Lapping, Lisa and Robert Loring, Achsah O'Donovan, Laurie Perzley, Fern Phillips, Andy Pitz, Kevin Rodel, Honor Fox Sage, Paul Sarli, Herman and Louise Stump,

Elizabeth Swain and Christopher Ayres, Roy Van Vleck, Minnie Watriss, Benson and Hartley Webster, Rosemary Whitney, Lindsay and Minot Weld, and my community in Pownal, Maine, who have kept me going.

To my succession of editors, all of whom appeared at precisely the right moment: Helen Whybrow, author and editor, who was a joy to work with, and from whom I learned so much; Amy MacDonald, author and community activist, who began by giving me early advice and, in a stroke of good luck, later turned to editing and copy editing; Melissa Hayes, final copy editor, with whom I struck up an instantaneous connection; and David Platt, newspaper and journal editor, whose stellar sense of humor and incisive fine tuning at the end helped the stories to flow their best.

To Matt Kania of Maphero, whose support and terrific maps gave context to each story.

To Tom Morgan and Laura McBride of Blue Design, whose talent is obvious, but whose patience and good humor toward a neophyte like me was exemplary.

And finally, to those I spoke to and worked with from each story, either in person, by phone, or e-mail, I treasured meeting every one of you— kindred spirits, all:

Portland Trails: Isabel Aley, Colin Baker, Jessica Burton, George Campbell, Kevin Carley, Jim Cohen, Nan Cumming, Abby King Diggins, Elizabeth Ehrenfeld, Charlotte Henderson, Bruce Hyman, Alex Jaegerman, Tom Jewell, Susy Kist, Bob Krug, Wendell Large, Donna Larson, David Littell, Steve Mohr, Peter Monro, Laura Newman, Rick Knowland, John Kevin O'Brien, Phil Poirier, George Potter, Rob Rosenthal, Nathan Smith, Dick Spencer, Phil Thompson, David Willauer, and Alessa Wylie.

Bronx River Restoration Project: Jenny Hoffner; and Brian Aucoin, Majora Carter, Linda Cox, Teresa Crimmens, Resa Dimino, Elyse Leon, Sylvia Rodriguez-Seda, Syieda Passe, Alexie Torres-Fleming, Kate Van Tassel, Dart Westphal, Brad Wier, and Ricardo Levins Morales—for the use of his beautiful and inspirational poster.

Canyon Lake Creek Community Forest: Rand Jack and Gordon Scott; and Connie Clement, Hilda Bajema, Rod Burton, Roger DeSpain, Katherine Freimond, Dana Jack, Bob Keller, Craig Lee, Trish Navarre, Russ Paul, Russ Pfeiffer-Hoyt, Bill Pope, Mike Ryan, and Wendy Walker.

Common Harvest Farm: Margaret Pennings and Dan Guenther; and Janet Anderson, Michelle Dingwall, Rick Gauger, Ann Gilbert and Dan Pederson, Amy Middleton, Mikki Nazelrod, Mindy Ahlers-Olmstead, Kraig Olmstead, Jo Anne Rohricht, Dan Sullivan, and Doug Wubben.

Rocky Mountain Front Advisory Committee: Dave Carr; and Lisa Bay, Stoney Burk, Dusty and Danelle Crary, Anne and Larry Dellwo, Lyle Hodgskiss, Tana Kappel, Karl and Teri Rappold, and Mary Sexton.

Vision 2000—The Tyrrell County Economic Development Initiative: Mikki Sager; and J.D. Brickhouse, Lee Brickhouse, Peggy Griffin, Carlisle Harrell, Michael Harrell, Mr. Henry

Hill, Mavis Hill, Simon Jones, Doris Maldonado, Marimar McNaughton, Brenda Mixon, Sara Phelps, Feather Phillips, Annette Reynolds, Alecia Rodgers, Tracy Spruill, Carl Twarog, and Jackie Peoples Woolard.

And Others From Whom I Drew Inspiration:
American Farmland Trust: Brian Gumm and Jennifer Vincent. Durham Community Land Trust, Durham, NC: Selina Mack. Etowah River Greenway, Canton, GA: Elizabeth Cole. National Park Service Rivers & Trails: Alison Bullock, Steve Bowes, Cate Bradley, Charlotte Gillis, Wink Hastings, Paul Labovitz, Ursula Lemansky, Robert Potter and Cassie Thomas. The Nature Conservancy: Holly Richter, Upper San Pedro, AZ; Dave Harris, Lower San Pedro, AZ; Tom Duffus, Duluth, MN; Larissa Barry, Christine Conte, Libby Ellis, and Rachel Maurer. Sunnyside Farms, Washington, VA: David Cole and Brian Cramer.

PHOTOGRAPHY AND ILLUSTRATION CREDITS

Bronx River Alliance: pages 8, 144, 151

Stoney Burk: pages 12, 92, 101, 114, 115, 117

Rod Burton: page 74

Jay Dusard, for The Nature Conservancy: page 94

Historic photographs from Portland, Maine: pages 25, 26, 45, 192, 194

Virginia Farley: pages 176, 179

Alix Hopkins: pages 20, 38, 49, 53–63, 65, 66, 77, 80–83, 86–88, 95, 97–99, 102, 105, 106, 110, 111, 113, 118, 121, 123, 125, 127, 128, 131, 133, 142, 143, 176, 177

Rand Jack/Whatcom Land Trust: 71, 73–75, 78, 85

Mike Kamber: page 158

Susy Kist: page 35

C. Michael Lewis illustrations: pages 16, 36

Ricardo Levins Morales, for Northland Poster Collective: page 150

Dominique Nabakov/Union Square Awards: page 153

National Park Service Rivers & Trails: pages 173, 174

Laura Newman: page 48

Pocosin Arts: pages 138–140

Phil Poirier: page 34

Portland Rotary: page 34

Colleen Pratt: page 170

Portland Trails: pages 2, 22, 27, 28, 32, 40, 47

Bill Redinger woodcut, for MACSAC: page 64

Alice Spencer: page 43

Jim Steinberg: page 109

Jeffrey Stevensen: pages 21, 202

The Conservation Fund: pages 131, 134

Charles Tracy: page 30

Whatcom County Parks & Recreation Department: pages 68, 78, 84

Stuart White, for The Nature Conservancy: page 91

Jerry Willis, for the National Park Service: pages 5, 10, 15, 147–149, 154–157, 159, 161–169, 182, 207

Woodcut for Common Harvest Farm: page 50